Fire Up!

A Bible Study of God's Holy Spirit

© 2018 LifeMark Ministries

All rights reserved. No portion of this book may be reproduced, stored in a retrieval system, or transmitted in any form or by any means – electronic, mechanical, photocopy, recording, scanning, or other – except for brief quotations in critical reviews or articles, without the prior written permission of the publisher. Requests for permission should be addressed in writing to:

LifeMark Publications

2001 W. Plano Parkway, Suite 3403

Plano, TX 75075

ISBN: 978-1-944058-03-6

Scripture quotations marked (NIV) are taken from the Holy Bible, New International Version®, NIV®. Copyright © 1973, 1978, 1984, 2011 by Biblica, Inc.™ Used by permission of Zondervan. All rights reserved worldwide. www.zondervan.com The "NIV" and "New International Version" are trademarks registered in the United States Patent and Trademark Office by Biblica, Inc.™

Design by Angeline Collier / Halo Creative
www.halocreative.com

Table of Contents

Fan the Flame: How to Cultivate a Lifestyle of Prayer i
Lesson 1: Who is the Holy Spirit? 2
Lesson 2: Special Appearances 6
Lesson 3: Unlikely Candidates 10
Lesson 4: God is Faithful! 14
Lesson 5: In the Middle of It All! 18
Lesson 6: The Curtain Rises 22
Lesson 7: The Apostles Get Fired Up! 26
Lesson 8: Shock and Awe 30
Lesson 9: Fire That Purifies 34
Lesson 10: The Bright Burn of a Bonfire 38
Lesson 11: The Fire Spreads: Stephen & Philip 42
Lesson 12: The Fire Spreads: Saul & Peter 46
Lesson 13: Advancements and Adversity Intertwined 50
Lesson 14: Born Again 56
Lesson 15: Illumination of the Spirit 60
Lesson 16: Muddy Waters: Baptism by the Holy Spirit 64
Lesson 17: Sealed by the Holy Spirit 70
Lesson 18: Filled with the Holy Spirit 74
Lesson 19: Walking with the Holy Spirit 78
Lesson 20: Where There's Smoke, There's Fire: Spiritual Fruit 82
Lesson 21: Where There's Smoke, There's Fire: Spiritual Gifts 88
Lesson 22: Looking for a Sign 92
Lesson 23: Viewing Today in Light of the Future 98
Lesson 24: How Then Shall We Live? 102
Notes 106
Conclusion 109
Additional Resources 110

A believer's **LifeMark** is the *legacy* left by a life spent *loving* and *serving* God and man.

LifeMark Ministries exists to help people discover that the Bible is *alive, active, and applicable.*
We help people *learn* God's Word so they can boldly *live* His Word...for His glory!
This is our calling and our passion. This is our LifeMark. What's yours?

To learn more about this ministry, visit our website: **www.LifeMarkMinistries.org**

LifeMark Ministries was founded by **Mark Schupbach**, a businessman with a desire to use the experience, gifts, and talents he has been given by God to support and equip believers in their faith journey.

Mark's involvement with the church and ministry began more than 30 years ago. He has served as an elder and president on three church governing boards in both Wichita, Kansas, and Dallas, Texas. He was involved in Bible Study Fellowship for 17 years, including serving as the Men's Teaching Leader in Dallas for 9 years. In 2003, Mark founded Next Step Bible Study to encourage participants to seek a deeper, more intimate relationship with the Lord Jesus Christ. With a firm reliance on the Holy Spirit, Mark enjoys exhorting believers to get out of their "comfort zones" and fulfill their purpose.

Mark has been married to his wife, Marty, since 1969. They have 3 married daughters and 6 grandchildren.

Jennifer Hicks has a diverse background in both business and ministry, and she enjoys using her experience to encourage others in their faith journey. Working with Mark since 2007, she is grateful to God for opportunities to use her gifts and skill sets in a wide variety of projects including the development of Bible study curriculum and online resources as well as the planning of LifeMark ministry events.

In addition to ministry endeavors, Jennifer enjoys capturing the special moments of life as a freelance photographer. She is a die-hard Aggie, enjoys discussing current events, and is passionate about all things sports (especially Aggie football!).

How to Use This Study

Each week you will complete the lesson preparation and then meet with your small group to review your lesson and watch The Talk (on video). Start your lesson preparation with prayer, asking God to open your eyes to see the lessons He has for you.

Each lesson is structured identically with the following sections:

Introduction - This section will help you understand the context of the lesson.

Questions - Answer these in preparation for each week's study.

Quotes and Did You Know? - Throughout the lessons, you will notice special boxes of background information that may help you in your lesson preparation.

Pyro Principles - List principles you learn in the study. A principle is a truth about God (His person, character, etc.), a promise or warning from God or a statement of how He relates to mankind.

Are You Fired Up? - As you complete the lesson, spend some time reflecting on specific, tangible steps you will take to apply what you've learned.

Fan the Flame - Cultivating a strong prayer life helps you engage the power of the Holy Spirit. On the following pages, you'll find some prayer tips and sample "prayer guides" to provide a framework for your daily prayer time if you don't already have one.

Notes from Mark's Talk - Take notes while you listen to "The Talk" by Mark Schupbach.

Key Verse - Ponder this verse daily and allow it to penetrate your heart and mind.

Keep in mind that this is a workbook, not a textbook. Don't be afraid to write in it, highlight it, circle key words – whatever it takes to help you absorb the content. We also recommend either purchasing a good Bible dictionary or using some online resources when you come across words or phrases with which you are not familiar. Here are a few web sites we recommend:

www.Bible.org

www.BlueLetterBible.org

www.GotQuestions.org

Before we get started, take a minute to write down what you hope to gain from this study:

_____

_____

_____

_____

Like anything, the more time and effort you invest in this study, the more you will grow in your walk with God. Most importantly, pray for God to guide you and for the Holy Spirit to reveal God's truth to you as you study and seek to apply His Word.

Acknowledgements

Dear Friend,

Thank you for joining us on this journey through God's Word as we learn more about His Holy Spirit together. Based on past experience and conversations with many of you, there is a general level of knowledge about God the Father and about His Son, Jesus Christ. However, when it comes to the Holy Spirit, people often times either don't know what they believe or don't know why they hold that belief.

However, the Bible has a lot to tell us about God's Holy Spirit. In fact, a Logos case-sensitive search of the word "Spirit" indicates there are 319 references occurring in 296 verses of the NASB. Obviously, this study cannot cover all of these verses, so we've done our best to guide you to discover exactly **what** you believe about the Spirit and equally important, **why**.

This study may stretch you at times, and that's ok. Don't be afraid to ask your leader follow-up questions. If they don't know the answer, they'll try to point you in the right direction. The Holy Spirit can be a difficult, complicated, and sometimes divisive topic, but at the same time, **He's a priceless gift from God!** It will be well-worth the investment of your time and energy to learn more about Him over the coming months and grow even deeper in your relationship with God as a result.

Before we begin, we'd like to take a moment to express our gratitude to a few individuals who greatly contributed to the development of this study:

- Dr. Timothy Warren — Thank you for being a fountain of knowledge and an excellent "coach" throughout the development of this study.

- Kathy Prather — Thank you for your eagle's eye in reviewing this study.

- Angeline Collier — Thank you for using your creative gifts to bring the text alive visually.

- A few editors who wish to remain anonymous — Thank you for contributing your time, energy, and experience to greatly improve the lessons.

Also, a special note of appreciation to Pastors Tom Rodgers and Reggie Coe — Thank you for living 2 Timothy 2:2 and for the incredible Biblical foundation you have given so many over the years. Tom was taken home to be with Jesus recently, but his impact and legacy will live on for generations through those He loved and taught so faithfully.

For God's glory,

LifeMark Ministries

How to Cultivate a Lifestyle of Prayer

"Rejoice always, pray continually, give thanks in all circumstances, for this is God's will for you in Christ Jesus." **1 Thessalonians 5:16-18 (NIV)**

We live in a society that thrives on being **constantly connected** — work emails, social media, Facetime, Skype, etc. Whether someone is in your own back yard or halfway around the world, constant connectivity is at an all-time high. Yet, staying constantly connected with God seems to be at an all-time low, doesn't it?

For many of us, prayer is something we do when we need something, when we're about to eat a meal, or right before we drift off to sleep. But the Bible encourages us to pray CONTINUALLY! What does that mean and how can we intentionally cultivate a **lifestyle of prayer**?

Well it starts with talking to the Lord **each day**. We recommend beginning your day this way — it will help frame your mindset from the very beginning and affect your perspective throughout the day. In this year's study workbook, we've added a few prayer tools to help you do this:

1) **Prayer Tips and "Kindling"** — We've reached out to some real "prayer warriors" in the LifeMark family and have collected their feedback for practical tips to help encourage you in your prayer journey.

2) **Prayer Trackers** — Spread over the next few pages are some charts to help you track your prayers. Feel free to use any of these to help cultivate your prayer lifestyle. We encourage you to tear these pages out, make copies, and create a prayer notebook so you'll have them going forward. It's important to recognize that your prayer time with the Lord is personal and relational, not a check-off list. However, having tangible reminders to help guide you and keep you accountable can be both encouraging and helpful! It's also encouraging to look back over time and see how God has answered many prayers that you probably won't even remember having prayed — **He is faithful!**

- **Ongoing Prayer Requests & Updates** — This page is designed for significant prayer requests that are ongoing in nature. For example, the salvation of a loved one, a personal health battle, the restoration of a broken relationship, etc. Simply write in your request and then as you have updates, make a note on the page and track the progress over time. This is also a great place to capture lessons God is teaching you through the "waiting" season!

- **Weekly Prayer Tracker** — This 2-page spread is designed to walk you through the traditional "A-C-T-S" steps of prayer on a daily basis. "ACTS" stands for: Adoration, Confession, Thanksgiving, and Supplication (which is just a fancy word for your requests!). Whether you write in the boxes or just use this page as a general outline for your prayer time, get in the habit of using this page each day — this will help you learn the discipline of intentional prayer more than anything else will!

- **General Prayer Guide** — This is designed for those of you who enjoy writing / journalling and want more space for the different sections of the "A-C-T-S" prayer model.

Prayer Tips & "Kindling"

Prayer Tips

1) Plan a regular time and place to pray — it should be private and away from the business of this world. Things like texts on your cell phone and to-do lists at your desk will interrupt your prayer time and before you know it, you'll be down a different path!

2) Start your prayer time with a song of praise or by reading some Scripture or a devotional. Psalms make great "prayer kindling," and we've listed some below to help you.

3) Try getting on your knees to pray — this may sounds strange at first, but there's something about doing a physical act of submission that reminds us of God's holiness and the reverence with which we should approach God when we pray.

4) Write down your thoughts — both your praises and your prayers! Keeping track helps you stay consistent and increases your awareness of God's involvement in your life. You'll begin to see His hand at work in ways that you didn't previously see…all because you are looking.

5) Don't be overwhelmed trying to pray the "correct" prayer…think of it as just a conversation with God. Take all your needs and concerns to Him, and LEAVE them with Him. He offers to bear our burdens for us — let Him!

If you will apply these tips, utilize these tools, and ask God to cultivate a lifestyle of prayer in your life, you will be amazed at the change you will see over time!

Prayer Kindling

Here are some passages that make great "prayer starters" so we will refer to them as "kindling" — choose one each day to help you begin your time of prayer with adoration to the Lord.

Psalm 3:1-6	**Psalm 47**	**Psalm 97**
Psalm 5:3-7, 11-12	**Psalm 53:8-9**	**Psalm 98**
Psalm 8:1-9	**Psalm 59:16-17**	**Psalm 100**
Psalm 9:1-11	**Psalm 65:5-13**	**Psalm 104**
Psalm 13:5-6	**Psalm 66**	**Psalm 105:1-7**
Psalm 16:5-11	**Psalm 68:3-10, 32-35**	**Psalm 111**
Psalm 18:1-3, 25-36	**Psalm 71:19-24**	**Psalm 113**
Psalm 19:1-9	**Psalm 72:18-19**	**Psalm 119:169-176**
Psalm 23	**Psalm 84**	**Psalm 121**
Psalm 28:6-9	**Psalm 86:5-13**	**Psalm 134**
Psalm 29	**Psalm 89:1-18**	**Psalm 135:1-7**
Psalm 33:1-15	**Psalm 90:14-17**	**Psalm 136:1-9**
Psalm 34	**Psalm 92:1-5**	**Psalm 145**
Psalm 40:1-5	**Psalm 93**	**Psalm 146**
Psalm 42:1-2	**Psalm 95:1-7**	**Psalm 148**
Psalm 46	**Psalm 96**	**Psalm 150**

Ongoing Prayer Requests and Updates

This page is designed to help you track the progress and the lessons you learn while praying for a specific request over an extended period of time.

Describe the request here: Today's Date:

Notes, updates, lessons learned, etc:	Date of Update:

Weekly Prayer Tracker

	Sunday	Monday	Tuesday
God, You are…			
I confess to You…			
I thank you for…			
I ask You for…			
General Requests Schedule	The church body, Christian ministries, LifeMark, your small group leaders and members	Family — immediate and extended; for salvation for those who haven't believed; for your influence in the family; for personal obedience so that God would bless future generations	Schools, children, teachers, foster care, orphans & their caregivers

Week of:

Wednesday	Thursday	Friday	Saturday
Those who serve our country — Military / First Responders / Emergency Personnel and their families	Local and state government, judges, legal system, social services.	Nation — government, leadership, revival & repentance, spiritual health, courage to stand for Him, protection from temptations and evil.	World — missionaries, persecuted Christians, Israel, refugees, and for spreading of the gospel to the ends of the earth!

General Prayer Guide

This page is designed for those of you who enjoy writing / journalling and want more space for the different sections of the "A-C-T-S" prayer model.

God, You are…

I confess to You…

I thank You for…

I ask You for…

Lesson 1: Who is the Holy Spirit?

Introduction

Most believers struggle with really understanding who or what the Holy Spirit is. Instead of that driving us to learn more, we pull away because we're uncomfortable with what we don't know. It's human nature! But we're more than human...as believers, we actually have the Holy Spirit LIVING INSIDE of us! Don't just brush over that statement...allow it to really sink in! And if He's living inside of each of us, don't you think we should introduce ourselves and get to know Him better?

Let's start at the beginning — **who is the Holy Spirit?** Keep in mind, this week's lesson will establish a framework for the picture of the Holy Spirit that will be revealed in God's Word throughout the study. Therefore, some of these passages and verses will be studied again in greater depth.

1. **Before we begin this study, take a moment to write down what you currently know and / or believe about the Holy Spirit. Even if you don't know much about Him, that's ok. Just write down what you do know.**

2. The Holy Spirit is a <u>person</u> and He has a personality! The dictionary defines "personality" as "the sum total of the physical, mental, emotional, and social characteristics of an individual."[1] In other words, "personality" is what a person thinks and feels as well as how the person behaves. How would you describe different aspects of the Holy Spirit's personality using the following verses?

   <u>Mental Aspects</u>

   • Isaiah 11:2

   • Romans 8:27

   • 1 Corinthians 2:9-11; Ephesians 1:17

   <u>Emotional Aspects</u>

   • Romans 15:30

   • Ephesians 4:30

   <u>Behavioral Aspects</u>

   • Acts 16:6-12

   • 1 Corinthians 12:7-11

3. The Holy Spirit is a <u>spirit</u> and can take on the form or representation of creation, including the elements. Note that this is not a contradiction of saying that the Holy Spirit is a person. Look up the following verses to learn more about the various physical representations He has taken:

   • Matthew 3:16

   • John 3:8; Acts 2:2

   • John 4:14; 7:38-39

   • Acts 2:3

Did you know?

The Hebrew word for "spirit" (רוּחַ) can also be translated as "breath." There are some passages in the Bible that are debated regarding whether they refer to the literal breath of God or to God's Holy Spirit. You will see these passages included in studies, books, and articles about the Holy Spirit, but many scholars agree that these verses likely are referring to God the Father, not His Holy Spirit.[2] Here are some examples: Job 27:3; 33:4; Psalm 33:6; 104:29-30

4. The Holy Spirit is <u>God</u>. This is one thing that sets the Holy Spirit apart from other spiritually empowered beings referenced in the Bible (for example, Satan, demons, angels, etc) — they are not God, and the Holy Spirit is! What do you learn from the following verses about the divine attributes, activities, and associations of the Holy Spirit?

   <u>Divine Attributes</u>

   • Genesis 1:2

   • 1 Corinthians 2:11-12

   • Psalm 139:7; 1 Corinthians 6:19-20

   • Romans 15:19

   • Luke 11:13

   • Isaiah 40:13

   <u>Divine Activities</u>

   • 2 Peter 1:21

   • Luke 1:35

   <u>Divine Associations</u>

   • Acts 5:3-4

   • Matthew 28:19; 1 Cor. 12:4-6; 2 Cor. 13:14

   • Acts 28:25-27; Isaiah 6:8-13

5. Which of the three descriptions of the Holy Spirit do you struggle to understand and / or accept the most (Person, Spirit, or God) and why?

6. Why do you think some believers tend to minimize the authority and power of the Holy Spirit?

 **Pyro Principles:**
What principles did you learn in this week's lesson? Remember, a principle is a truth about God (His person, character, etc.), a promise or warning from God, or a statement of how He relates to mankind.

 *Are you fired up?*
What changes did this week's lesson **spark** in your life?

 Fan the Flame
Spend time each day intentionally asking God to help you apply what you've learned in this lesson. Refer to the prayer tips at the beginning of this workbook to provide a framework for your prayer time if you don't already have one. Cultivating a strong prayer life helps you engage the power of the Holy Spirit!

 *Talk Notes:*

 *"Who can fathom the Spirit of the Lord, or instruct the Lord as his counselor?" Isaiah 40:13 (NIV)*

Lesson 2: Special Appearances

Introduction:

Now that you have a better understanding of WHO the Holy Spirit is, let's take a look at some of His appearances in the Old Testament and discover what we can learn from them.

1. **What activity of the Holy Spirit that occurs throughout both the Old and New Testament is described in 2 Peter 1:20-21?**

2. **How does that knowledge affect your view of the Bible?**

3. **The Holy Spirit was involved from the very beginning of time. Describe his activities in the following verses:**

   • Genesis 1:2, 26

   • Genesis 6:1-8

- **Genesis 11:1-9**

- **Genesis 41:33-40**

- **Exodus 31:1-5**

- **Isaiah 63:9-14**

- **Judges 3:7-11**

- **2 Chronicles 24:17-22**

- **Nehemiah 9:16-21**

- **Micah 3:5-8**

> "Biblical inspiration may be defined as God's superintending human authors so that, using their own individual personalities, they composed and recorded without error His message to man in the words of their original writings in the Bible."
>
> — Charles Ryrie[3]

4. **What did God do in Numbers 11:16-25?**

5. **What purpose did the one-time gift of prophecy serve? (Numbers 11:25)**

6. What did Moses mean by what he said in Numbers 11:29?

7. How and when was his desire fulfilled? (Acts 1:5; 2:1-21)

8. In addition to the prophesied Messiah, God told the nation of Israel to watch for the work He would do *through His Holy Spirit*. What were some of these prophesies?

 • Isaiah 32:12-20; 44:1-5

 • Ezekiel 36:22-32; 37:1-14

 • Joel 2:28-32

 • Zechariah 12:10

Pyro Principles:
What principles did you learn in this week's lesson? Remember, a principle is a truth about God (His person, character, etc.), a promise or warning from God, or a statement of how He relates to mankind.

Are you fired up?
What changes did this week's lesson **spark** in your life?

Fan the Flame
Spend time each day intentionally asking God to help you apply what you've learned in this lesson. Refer to the prayer tips at the beginning of this workbook to provide a framework for your prayer time if you don't already have one. Cultivating a strong prayer life helps you engage the power of the Holy Spirit!

Talk Notes:

"For prophecy never had its origin in the human will, but prophets, though human, spoke from God as they were carried along by the Holy Spirit." 2 Peter 1:21 (NIV)

Lesson 3: Unlikely Candidates

Introduction:

Sometimes God sent His Holy Spirit to accomplish specific purposes through very unlikely people. This week, we'll take a look at some of these people and discover new insights about how God works supernaturally in unexpected ways.

Balaam

1. How would you describe Balaam's "spirituality"? (Numbers 22:6-8; 24:1-4; 2 Peter 2:1-22; Revelation 2:14)

2. What purpose did Balaam serve in Numbers 22:38 and Numbers 23:5, 12, 16, & 26?

    > "From the top of Peor, Balaam began with pagan acts of worship, but then he abandoned them and the Spirit of God came upon him. This was a most remarkable thing, considering that Balaam was not a man of true faith. The word of God is truth no matter how, or through whom, it is delivered!"
    >
    > — David Jeremiah[4]

3. What do you learn about God and how He disperses His Spirit from this story? (Numbers 24:2)

4. What promises did God make to the nation of Israel regarding their <u>disobedience</u>? (Jeremiah 25:8-14)

5. What promises did God make to the nation of Israel regarding their <u>obedience</u>? (Jeremiah 29:10-14)

6. Who was Cyrus? (Ezra 1:1-4; you may also find it beneficial to consult a Bible dictionary or online resource for additional details)

> "Although the Jews regarded Cyrus as a benefactor, as well they might, it should be noted that his 'beneficence' was not directed solely toward the Jews, but formed part of a wider foreign policy. The Cyrus Cylinder, in which Cyrus decrees that some exiled populations can return, mentions a number of deities and peoples whom he restored to their own places. The thinking behind this, no doubt, was to foster goodwill among the subjects of his kingdom."
>
> Cultural Backgrounds Study Bible[5]

7. How did God use His Spirit through Cyrus to fulfill these promises, and what do you learn from this? (Isaiah 44:28; 45:1, 13; Ezra 1:1-11)

8. Why did God do this? (Isaiah 45:3-7)

9. Who was Saul? (1 Samuel 9:1-2, 14-17, 21)

10. What do you learn from Samuel's actions and instructions to Saul in 1 Samuel 10:1, 6-7, 9-10?

11. Describe the changes in Saul personally and in his relationship with God. (1 Samuel 15:1-3, 9-12; 22:17-19)

12. How did God respond to Saul's disobedience? (1 Samuel 15:23; 16:1, 12-14; 18:12)

13. What do you learn about God's Holy Spirit from this story?

 **Pyro Principles:**
What principles did you learn in this week's lesson? Remember, a principle is a truth about God (His person, character, etc.), a promise or warning from God, or a statement of how He relates to mankind.

 ***Are you fired up?***
What changes did this week's lesson **spark** in your life?

 Fan the Flame
Spend time each day intentionally asking God to help you apply what you've learned in this lesson. Refer to the prayer tips at the beginning of this workbook to provide a framework for your prayer time if you don't already have one. Cultivating a strong prayer life helps you engage the power of the Holy Spirit!

 ***Talk Notes:***

 "'For my thoughts are not your thoughts, neither are your ways my ways,' declares the Lord."
- Isaiah 55:8 (NIV)

Lesson 4: God is Faithful!

Introduction:

Last week we talked about the appearances of the Holy Spirit in a few "unlikely" people in the Old Testament. This week, let's take a look at the presence of the Holy Spirit in two more men: one who was set apart from birth for service to the Lord and one who was known as "a man after God's own heart."

At first glance, these men seem to be more "likely" candidates for being filled with the Holy Spirit than the ones we studied last week, but as we'll discover, they were still human and allowed the lusts of the flesh to guide some of their decisions. Despite this, in both cases, God's Holy Spirit accomplished His will.

Samson

1. **What set Samson apart? In other words, how was he different from the average man? (Judges 13:4-5)**

    > "These are some of the saddest words in the Bible: The Lord had departed from him (Numbers 14: 42-43). This time, the now-pathetic Samson was paraded through the city, a picture of helplessness. He went from a champion of the Israelites to a prisoner in the Philistine camp and a slave to his own sin. Sadly the man who lived according to what was right in his eyes (Judges 14:2-3) lost his eyesight."
    >
    > — David Jeremiah[6]

2. **What is the Nazarite vow and what was the purpose of it? (Numbers 6:1-21)**

3. **What role(s) did the Holy Spirit play in Samson's life? (Judges 13:25; 14:6; 15:14)**

4. **Give some examples of ways that Samson broke his Nazarite vow. (Judges 14:1-10, 19; 15:8-15; 16:4)**

5. Why did the cutting of Samson's hair lead to his loss of power? (Numbers 6:5, 13a, 18; Judges 16:16-20)

> "But the silver lining in all this is that, despite the mayhem, Yahweh's Spirit was at work, and for the first time, the Philistines are actually attacked by the judge-deliverer, Samson (14:19). The cause-and-effect relationship is clear: the movement of the Spirit leads to a mini-war against the Philistines at Ashkelon…"
>
> — Abraham Kuruvilla[7]

6. Why did Samson's strength return? (Judges 16:22, 28)

7. What was God's purpose for Samson's life, and in what ways did He accomplish that purpose despite Samson's poor choices? (Judges 13:5; 14:4; 16:30)

David

8. Describe the process of God selecting David as King, especially what happened to him in the last verse of 1 Samuel 16:1-13.

9. How did God reinforce His selection of David as King when he fought against Saul in 1 Chronicles 12:18?

10. How was David able to prophesy and what do you learn about God's Spirit from these verses? (2 Samuel 23:2-4; Matthew 22:41-46; Acts 1:15-17; Acts 4:25)

11. What was David's fear in Psalm 51:11 and why was he concerned? (2 Samuel 12:7-10)

12. What does his concern tell you about the presence of God's Spirit in the Old Testament?

13. How did the Spirit of God work through David in 1 Chronicles 28:6, 11-12?

14. What do you learn about the Spirit from David's description in 1 Chronicles 28:13-19?

15. When David came to the end of his life and reflected on it, how did he describe his relationship with God at the end and what do you learn from this? (2 Samuel 23:1-7)

 **Pyro Principles:**
What principles did you learn in this week's lesson? Remember, a principle is a truth about God (His person, character, etc.), a promise or warning from God, or a statement of how He relates to mankind.

 *Are you fired up?*
What changes did this week's lesson **spark** in your life?

 Fan the Flame
Spend time each day intentionally asking God to help you apply what you've learned in this lesson. Refer to the prayer tips at the beginning of this workbook to provide a framework for your prayer time if you don't already have one. Cultivating a strong prayer life helps you engage the power of the Holy Spirit!

Talk Notes:

 "...he who began a good work in you will carry it on to completion until the day of Christ Jesus."
- Philippians 1:6 (NIV)

Lesson 5: *In the Middle of It All!*

Introduction:

As we've read previously, the Holy Spirit warned the nation of Israel repeatedly through the prophets to turn from their wicked ways and repent before the Lord. However, the Jewish people were hard-hearted, stiff-necked, and rebellious. They suffered a lengthy and meaningful silence from God after they persecuted and killed His prophets (end of the Old Testament).

After about 400 years of persecution and nomadic living, the silence from heaven must have spoken volumes. A lot happened in this region during those 400 years — kings conquered and ruled, Greek society infiltrated and influenced, and new groups of religious leaders called Sadducees, Pharisees, and the Sanhedrin formed in the Jewish nation.

And then...God sent another prophet — a man named John the Baptist — to break that silence with a bold proclamation: "Prepare the way for the Lord, make straight paths for Him." Not only was God speaking to the people through His Spirit again, He was announcing the arrival of the anticipated Messiah! WOW!

This week, we'll take a closer look at some of the appearances of the Holy Spirit in the gospels. You may be surprised to learn that He's really in the middle of it all, pointing all eyes to Jesus!

1. **In what ways was the Holy Spirit active in the period of time around Jesus' birth?**

   • **Luke 1:35-36**

   • **Luke 1:15**

   • **Luke 1:41, 67**

   • **Luke 2:25**

> "Simeon, who was controlled, counseled, and conditioned by the Spirit of God, received the revelation concerning Christ in the same way that Jesus reveals Himself today: He was in the Scriptures, he knew the prophecies of the OT, and he was a man of prayer. That Simeon blessed God shows that he knew immediately, absolutely, and with authority that this was the Messiah."
>
> — David Jeremiah[8]

2. In what ways was the Holy Spirit active during the lifetime of Jesus?

　• Matthew 3:13-17; John 1:29-34; Acts 10:36-38

　• Matthew 4:1; Luke 4:1-2

　• Matthew 16:13-20; I Corinthians 12:1-3

　• Luke 10:21

3. How is the Holy Spirit (who would "rest upon" Jesus) described in Isaiah 11:1-2?

4. According to John 16:7-15, why did Jesus have to leave the earth and why would it be better for the disciples?

5. What promises did Jesus make to His disciples about the coming Holy Spirit (John 14:12-27; John 15:26-27)?

6. Explain the significance described in John 14:16 of how the Holy Spirit would be with the disciples in contrast to how the Holy Spirit worked in the Old Testament.

7. What phrase is used to describe the Holy Spirit in John 14:17a and John 15:26?

8. How does this affect your worship of God? Specifically, how does the Holy Spirit transform your worship of God? (John 4:23-24; Ephesians 4:18-20; Colossians 3:15-17)

9. What instructions did Jesus give His disciples before He ascended? (Matthew 28:16-20)

10. What did Jesus promise them at the end of Matthew 28:20, and how would that promise be fulfilled shortly after He ascended? (Acts 1:1-5)

11. What comfort does that promise give you?

Pyro Principles:
What principles did you learn in this week's lesson? Remember, a principle is a truth about God (His person, character, etc.), a promise or warning from God, or a statement of how He relates to mankind.

Are you fired up?
What changes did this week's lesson **spark** in your life?

Fan the Flame
Spend time each day intentionally asking God to help you apply what you've learned in this lesson. Refer to the prayer tips at the beginning of this workbook to provide a framework for your prayer time if you don't already have one. Cultivating a strong prayer life helps you engage the power of the Holy Spirit!

Talk Notes:

"When the Advocate comes, whom I will send to you from the Father — the Spirit of truth who goes out from the Father — he will testify about me." John 15:26 (NIV)

Lesson 6: The Curtain Rises

Introduction:

We ended last week's lesson with Jesus promising the gift of another advocate for all believers to receive after He left this earth. This is one of the purposes of the book of Acts — to tell the story of the early church after the powerful debut of the Holy Spirit on earth. Although He had made appearances throughout history, never before was His presence experienced in the hearts of ALL believers. For the next several weeks, we'll look at the Spirit's involvement in the early church and the impact He made in the radical transformation of Jesus' followers.

1. Where did Jesus tell the disciples to wait for the Holy Spirit? (Acts 1:4)

2. How did Jesus describe the Holy Spirit in Acts 1:4?

3. What contrast did Jesus make in Acts 1:5?

> "Before the day of Pentecost, the emphasis was on the word **ask** (see Luke 11:13). After Pentecost, the emphasis was on the word **receive** (see Acts 2:38). This is the good news: we are no longer waiting for the Holy Spirit — He is waiting for us. We are no longer living in a time of promise, but in the days of fulfillment."
>
> — Billy Graham[9]

4. What would the disciples receive when the Holy Spirit came, and what would it equip them to do? (Acts 1:8)

5. Do you fully engage the power of the Holy Spirit when sharing the gospel with others? If not, what steps can you take to change?

6. Where were the disciples when Jesus ascended into Heaven and what other significant events transpired near this location? (Acts 1:12; John 11:1-4; 12:1-3; Luke 19:28-44; 21:37-38; 22:39-46)

7. Describe the future significant event that is expected to happen at this location. (Acts 1:10-11; Zechariah 14:1-4; Matthew 24:26-31)

8. While the disciples followed Jesus' instructions to wait in Jerusalem, how did they spend their time? (Acts 1:12-26)

9. When you are in a "waiting season," how can you best utilize the time? (Philippians 4:6-7; Colossians 4:2)

10. How was the Holy Spirit involved in the process of replacing Judas? (Acts 1:16, 20, 24-26)

11. What lessons can you learn from Peter's example, and how can you apply them in your life?

12. What lessons can you learn from Barsabbas and Matthias, and how can you apply them in your life?

13. How can you apply James 4:6-10 and Matthew 23:11-12 in your life?

 **Pyro Principles:**
What principles did you learn in this week's lesson? Remember, a principle is a truth about God (His person, character, etc.), a promise or warning from God, or a statement of how He relates to mankind.

 *Are you fired up?*
What changes did this week's lesson **spark** in your life?

 Fan the Flame
Spend time each day intentionally asking God to help you apply what you've learned in this lesson. Refer to the prayer tips at the beginning of this workbook to provide a framework for your prayer time if you don't already have one. Cultivating a strong prayer life helps you engage the power of the Holy Spirit!

 *Talk Notes:*

 "But you will receive power when the Holy Spirit comes on you; and you will be my witnesses in Jerusalem, and in all Judea and Samaria, and to the ends of the earth." Acts 1:8 (NIV)

Lesson 7: The Apostles Get Fired Up!

Introduction:

The day they had anticipated had finally arrived! In their obedience to Jesus' command (and possibly still experiencing some fear about being persecuted or killed), the apostles waited together in a home. Jesus had prepared them as best He could with their limited understanding, but the supernatural transformation that occurs as a result of the promised gift of the Spirit is beyond anything they could have imagined! This week, we'll watch the apostles get "fired up" and observe the changes in them and in the believers who followed their leadership. Then we'll study the activities of the early church and how we can learn from their example.

1. **Describe the scene in Acts 2:1-4.**

2. **What did it mean that they could "speak in tongues" in Acts 2:4, 6-8, and 11? What did it not mean?**

   > "In Matthew 16:18, He [Jesus] said: 'I will build My church and the gates of hell shall not prevail against it.' Acts is a fantastic book, because in it we see Him doing just that, and we find encouragement to participate in His great program of church building."
   >
   > Dr. Thomas L. Constable[10]

3. **What do you learn about God, His plan, and His timing from Acts 2:5?**

26

4. What were the two responses of those observing this supernatural event, and why were they radically different?

5. What does Peter use in his rebuttal to the hecklers, and what do you learn from this? (Acts 2:15-21, 25-28; Isaiah 55:6-11)

6. What does Christ's resurrection give believers and why? (Acts 2:25-27)

7. What do you learn about the Holy Spirit from Acts 2:32-33?

8. How did the people respond to Peter's admonition? (Acts 2:37)

9. What instructions and promises did Peter give them in Acts 2:38-39?

10. What was Peter's focus and what was the result?

11. What did these new believers do with their time? (Acts 2:42-47a)

12. What was the result of these activities? (Acts 2:47b)

> "The Holy Spirit is mentioned in the Book of Acts more than 50 times. Any attempted work of the church is doomed to failure without the Spirit (John 16:7-11)."
>
> — David Jeremiah[11]

13. Are you excited about Jesus like the early church believers were? Do you incorporate what God has done in your life regularly in your conversations? If not, what happened to dampen your excitement and what steps can you take to get it back?

14. What steps can you take to release the Holy Spirit in your church in order to have the powerful, transformative impact of the early church?

Pyro Principles:
What principles did you learn in this week's lesson? Remember, a principle is a truth about God (His person, character, etc.), a promise or warning from God, or a statement of how He relates to mankind.

Are you fired up?
What changes did this week's lesson **spark** in your life?

Fan the Flame
Spend time each day intentionally asking God to help you apply what you've learned in this lesson. Refer to the prayer tips at the beginning of this workbook to provide a framework for your prayer time if you don't already have one. Cultivating a strong prayer life helps you engage the power of the Holy Spirit!

Talk Notes:

"Repent and be baptized, every one of you, in the name of Jesus Christ for the forgiveness of your sins. And you will receive the gift of the Holy Spirit." Acts 2:38 (NIV)

Lesson 8: Shock and Awe

Introduction:

Now that the church has been established and is growing and spreading rapidly, they begin to face opposition. This week's lesson begins with a man who had been lame since birth. When you consider that he was in Jerusalem, in the center of all that had transpired over the last few years with Jesus' ministry, death, and resurrection, it's likely that he had heard stories about Him.

Did he believe what he'd been told? Did his friends ever try to take him to meet Jesus with the hope that he would be healed? Now that Jesus had died, perhaps this man had lost hope and resigned himself to the life he'd always known. We aren't told much about him but allow yourself to consider his circumstances as you read his story. . .

1. What did the lame man ask for in Acts 3:1-10, and what did he receive?

2. Is there something in your life that you struggle to pray about? Perhaps it seems too big or you feel unworthy. Or perhaps your struggle points to a deeper issue that you simply don't want to address right now.

3. How can the Holy Spirit help you overcome this struggle? (Ephesians 3:14-21; Romans 8:26-28)

4. How long did the actual act of healing take? What did the lame man do afterwards and where did he do it? (Acts 3:7-8)

5. How does Peter explain the miracle healing? (Acts 3:12-16; Matthew 28:18)

> **Did you know?**
>
> Solomon's Colonnade or "the porch called Solomon's" referred to a part of the temple complex build by King Herod. It had a cedar roof supported by double white marble columns that were approximately 38 feet tall. This colonnade provided a natural place for crowds to gather and people to teach. Jesus taught there in John 10:23 and the early church frequently gathered there as well as described in Acts 3:11 and 5:12.

6. Who was in the crowd that day, listening to Peter's comments? Who joined them the following day after Peter and John spent the night in prison? (Acts 4:1, 5-6)

7. What was significant about these men? (John 18:12-14, 24, 28)

8. Given Peter's experience in John 18:15-18 and 25-27, how would you have *expected* him to respond to being arrested and brought before these powerful men?

9. How did Peter *actually* respond? (Acts 4:7-12)

10. Explain the change in Peter. (Luke 22:31; John 14:15-21; 17:14-19; 21:15-19)

11. How did the leaders see Peter and John and to whom did they credit the change? (Acts 4:13)

12. Are people amazed by your courage and boldness? Do they know the source of your strength? If not, what steps can you take to change this?

13. How did the Jewish leaders plan to stop Jesus' impact from spreading? (Acts 4:16-18)

14. What does that tell you about Jesus' name? (Acts 4:10,12; Philippians 2:9-11; Luke 10:17; John 3:18; 14:13-14; Romans 10:13)

15. How did Peter and John reply to the threats made by the Jewish leaders, and how can you apply this in your own life? (Acts 4:19-20; Matthew 10:28)

 **Pyro Principles:**
What principles did you learn in this week's lesson? Remember, a principle is a truth about God (His person, character, etc.), a promise or warning from God, or a statement of how He relates to mankind.

 *Are you fired up?*
What changes did this week's lesson **spark** in your life?

 Fan the Flame
Spend time each day intentionally asking God to help you apply what you've learned in this lesson. Refer to the prayer tips at the beginning of this workbook to provide a framework for your prayer time if you don't already have one. Cultivating a strong prayer life helps you engage the power of the Holy Spirit!

 *Talk Notes:*

 "Now to him who is able to do immeasurably more than all we ask or imagine, according to his power that is at work within us, to him be glory in the church and in Christ Jesus throughout all generations, for ever and ever!"
Ephesians 3:20-21 (NIV)

Lesson 9: *Fire That Purifies*

Introduction:

What happens when the fire on a stovetop is increased? The substance in the pot can respond in different ways. Sometimes, it's purified (like in the case of boiling water). Other times, it burns. In a similar fashion, as the fire of the Holy Spirit increased in the early church, the "heat" increased, too. Sinful behavior and impure motives crept in, and actions that grieved and squelched the impact of the Holy Spirit had to be addressed and purged for the protection of the church.

1. **When Peter and John returned to their fellow believers and shared what happened, how did the people respond? (Acts 4:23-24)**

2. **What did they ask God for, and what did they NOT ask Him for that one might have expected? (Acts 4:29-30)**

3. **How did God answer their prayers and what do you learn from this? (Acts 4:31; Matthew 7:7-11)**

4. **In what ways do you see the presence of the Holy Spirit in the church at that time? (Acts 4:31-35)**

5. What do you learn about the man named Joseph from Acts 4:36 and Acts 11:22-24?

6. Ananias and Sapphira were also among the believers who sold property to help provide for the needs of the church body. However, their story is quite different. What did they decide to do in Acts 5:1-2?

7. What do you learn from Acts 5:3 about the spiritual battle that rages in the souls of believers and what are some tangible steps you can take to win that battle? (1 Peter 5:6-9)

> "When he [Satan] failed to destroy the early church, he tried to infiltrate and hinder it by prompting people to live in insincere and hypocritical ways. He still uses such tactics today."
>
> David Jeremiah[12]

8. How is this spiritual battle described in 1 Peter 5:6-9, and what tangible steps you can take to win that battle?

9. What happened to Ananias and Sapphira, and how did the people respond? (Acts 5:5-6, 10-11)

10. What do you learn about the Holy Spirit from this story?

11. Using a dictionary or online resource, define the words "grieve" and "quench."

12. How do we grieve the Holy Spirit? (Ephesians 4:17-30)

13. What can you deduce from the truth that the Holy Spirit grieves when we disobey the Lord? What does that tell you about the Holy Spirit's feelings toward God and believers?

14. How does a lifestyle that repeatedly grieves the Holy Spirit affect our spiritual life? (Psalm 66:16-20; Isaiah 59: 2)

15. What actions can we take to avoid quenching the Spirit? (1 Thessalonians 5:16-24)

 **Pyro Principles:**
What principles did you learn in this week's lesson? Remember, a principle is a truth about God (His person, character, etc.), a promise or warning from God, or a statement of how He relates to mankind.

 *Are you fired up?*
What changes did this week's lesson **spark** in your life?

 **Fan the Flame**
Spend time each day intentionally asking God to help you apply what you've learned in this lesson. Refer to the prayer tips at the beginning of this workbook to provide a framework for your prayer time if you don't already have one. Cultivating a strong prayer life helps you engage the power of the Holy Spirit!

 Talk Notes:

 "Rejoice always, pray continually, give thanks in all circumstances; for this is God's will for you in Christ Jesus." 1 Thessalonians 5:16-18 (NIV)

Lesson 10: The Bright Burn of a Bonfire

Introduction:

Have you ever experienced a bonfire? Perhaps at camp or at a school pep rally or a party? The fire is incredibly hot and powerful — some would say it's frighteningly so! At the same time, it's mesmerizing, too. The glow from large bonfires can be seen from far distances, drawing people to discover the light source.

The early church burned with the light of Christ like a powerful bonfire because of the Holy Spirit. Also like a bonfire, the early church fed off its own heat and grew larger and despite the attempts by the Sanhedrin to squelch it. This week, we'll learn more about those attempts and how the apostles responded.

1. **Compare Acts 5:12-16 with Matthew 17:14-21. What similarities and differences do you notice?**

2. **What does this tell you about the Holy Spirit?**

> "Within the darkness of life, God remains awake and aware (Psalm 121:2-4). No prison, no suffering, no lonely desert is beyond His presence (Hebrews 13:5)."
>
> — David Jeremiah[13]

3. **After the apostles were arrested in Acts 5:18, what happened and how did they respond?**

4. When the Jewish leaders confronted the apostles in Acts 5:28, what issue did they challenge them about?

5. What obvious question did the Jewish leaders NOT ask, and what does this tell you about their state of mind?

6. Why were the Jewish leaders concerned about the influence of the apostles teaching in the name of Jesus? (Acts 5:17, 28)

7. Have you ever been caught in a situation where man was telling you something that was contradictory to God's instructions to you? How did you respond and what did you learn from this experience?

8. How did Peter and the apostles reply in Acts 5:29-32?

9. Why would this have infuriated the Jewish leaders even more? (Acts 5:17, 32; Hebrews 7:23-28)

10. What argument did the Pharisee named Gamaliel make in Acts 5:33-39?

11. How did the Jewish leadership respond to Gamaliel's counsel in Acts 5:40?

12. Describe the response of the apostles in Acts 5:41-42.

13. How was the Holy Spirit likely involved in their response? (John 14:25-26; Matthew 5:10-12)

14. What difficulty are you experiencing right now and how can you follow the example set by the apostles? You likely are not facing direct persecution for your faith like they did, but you very well might be facing the effects of spiritual warfare and the consequences of living in a fallen, sinful world. (1 Peter 4:12-19)

 ### Pyro Principles:
What principles did you learn in this week's lesson? Remember, a principle is a truth about God (His person, character, etc.), a promise or warning from God, or a statement of how He relates to mankind.

What changes did this week's lesson **spark** in your life?

 ### Fan the Flame
Spend time each day intentionally asking God to help you apply what you've learned in this lesson. Refer to the prayer tips at the beginning of this workbook to provide a framework for your prayer time if you don't already have one. Cultivating a strong prayer life helps you engage the power of the Holy Spirit!

 ### Talk Notes:

 "Blessed are you when people insult you, persecute you, and falsely say all kinds of evil against you because of me." Matthew 5:11 (NIV)

Lesson 11: The Fire Spreads: Stephen & Philip

Introduction:

With the growth of the early church, new problems and needs began to arise, dividing some among them. The twelve apostles sought to delegate authority to God-fearing believers so that they could remain focused on prayer and the ministry of the Word of God. Two such men were Stephen and Philip, on whom we focus in this week's lesson.

Interestingly, all seven men who were selected had Greek names which meant they were most likely all Hellenistic Jews, the Greek minority of Jews who had migrated to Jerusalem. This was the group who felt they were being treated unfairly. In other words, the Hebrew majority selected seven leaders from the Greek minority to solve the problem.

1. How was Stephen described in Acts 6:3-5, 8?

2. According to Acts 6:7, as the Word of God spread, what two things happened as a result? (Ezekiel 36:26-27)

3. How was Stephen able to argue successfully against those who opposed him? (Luke 21:12-19; Acts 6:10)

4. With the increasing attacks on Christianity in the public square, does fear of persecution ever prevent you from publicly proclaiming your faith?

5. What can you learn from Stephen's example? (Matthew 6:34)

6. Stephen proceeded to recount Jewish history, and then he directly confronted the Jewish leaders. What did he say that infuriated them in Acts 7:51-54?

7. What did Stephen see, and why did his description lead the Sanhedrin to stone him?

8. In what ways did Stephen follow Jesus' example? (Matthew 5:43-48; 16:24-26; Luke 23:34, 46)

9. What happened that same day according to Acts 8:1? What good resulted from this and what do you learn from it? (Acts 1:8; 8:4; Genesis 50:20)

10. How was the apostles' response different in Acts 8:1 than in Matthew 26:56, and to whom do you credit that difference?

11. How was Philip described in Acts 6:3, 21:8-9?

12. What do you learn from the example of Simon the Sorcerer? (Acts 8:9-14, 18-24; Matthew 13:1-9, 18-23; Jeremiah 17:9-10)

13. The delayed receipt of the Holy Spirit by the Samaritans is a unique set of circumstances. Considering the antipathy between the Samaritans and the Jews, what blessings came about from this experience? (Acts 8:14-17)

> *"History reveals that Simon's faith was not genuine; he was just amazed by Philip's miracles. Simon became known as Simon Magus and was a leading heretic in the second century. Mentioned in the writings of the early church as one who claimed to be the incarnation of the highest god, he was ultimately the father of the biggest threat Christianity faced in the first 200 (and beyond) years of its life: Gnosticism."*
>
> David Jeremiah[14]

14. How is the story of the Ethiopian eunuch different from Simon's story? (Acts 8:26-40)

15. How can you follow Philip's example in Acts 8:35?

16. How did the Holy Spirit work through Philip to save the Ethiopian eunuch?

 **Pyro Principles:**
What principles did you learn in this week's lesson? Remember, a principle is a truth about God (His person, character, etc.), a promise or warning from God, or a statement of how He relates to mankind.

 *Are you fired up?*
What changes did this week's lesson **spark** in your life?

 **Fan the Flame**
Spend time each day intentionally asking God to help you apply what you've learned in this lesson. Refer to the prayer tips at the beginning of this workbook to provide a framework for your prayer time if you don't already have one. Cultivating a strong prayer life helps you engage the power of the Holy Spirit!

 Talk Notes:

 "Enter through the narrow gate. For wide is the gate and broad is the road that leads to destruction, and many enter through it. But small is the gate and narrow the road that leads to life, and only a few find it."
Matthew 7:13-14 (NIV)

Lesson 12: The Fire Spreads: Saul & Peter

Introduction:

The story of Saul's conversion was so significant that apart from the death, burial, and resurrection of Christ, this story is longer and told more often than any other in the New Testament. This makes sense given how supernatural the conversion was: from the most violent and powerful terrorist against Christianity to the most passionate and powerful evangelist for Christianity! Not to mention, the majority of the non-gospel books in the New Testament were written by Paul after his conversion.

We've already studied Peter's radical transformation after being filled with the Holy Spirit, but this week, we'll see how God stretched his faith again by redirecting him to minister to the Gentiles.

The Spirit of God changed the "sight" of both men and prepared them to be used supernaturally in the growth of the early church. Their effect extends to us, even today, as we learn from their teaching and their example.

1. **What do you learn about Saul from Acts 8:1, 3 and Acts 9:1-2?**

2. **What happened to Saul in Acts 9:3-9?**

3. **What did God restore through Ananias' hands and what was the result? (Acts 9:17-20)**

4. **What message did Saul preach, and how did the Jews who heard him respond? (Acts 9:20-25)**

5. How did Barnabas help Saul and how can you follow his example? (Acts 9:26-30)

6. What happened to the church after Saul's conversion, and what role did the Holy Spirit have? (Acts 9:31)

7. Peter continued healing others physically in the name of Jesus Christ, resulting in masses of people placing their faith in Jesus for their salvation. After healing Aeneas and Dorcas, Peter stayed in Joppa (Acts 9:32-43). While there, Peter had a vision. Describe this vision as detailed in Acts 10:9-16.

8. What do you learn about Cornelius from Acts 10:1-8?

> **Did you know?**
>
> Joppa was about 30 miles south of Caesarea — that was a lot of ground to cover in less than 24 hours, regardless of whether they were on foot or horseback!

9. How did Peter know that the men were looking for him, and what instructions did he receive? (Acts 10:17-20)

10. How did this experience change Peter and the circumcised believers who had traveled with him? (Acts 10:27-48)

11. What did Peter conclude about the two baptisms mentioned in Acts 10:47-48 and Acts 11:16? *Note that we will cover baptism in greater depth later in this study.*

12. How did Peter's experience impact other Jewish believers in the short-term? (Acts 11:1-4, 15-18)

13. How did Peter's experience impact other Jewish believers in the long-term? (Galatians 2:1-10; Ephesians 2:11-22)

14. God could have converted Saul immediately on the road to Damascus or sent Jesus in a vision to Cornelius and his family. Instead, God involved Ananias, Peter, and other believers in the conversions of these two men and those around them. Why does God work through mankind, and how do we benefit as a result?

15. When has God called you out of your comfort zone in order to fulfill His will? In what ways did that experience prepare you for something in the future?

Pyro Principles:
What principles did you learn in this week's lesson? Remember, a principle is a truth about God (His person, character, etc.), a promise or warning from God, or a statement of how He relates to mankind.

Are you fired up?
What changes did this week's lesson **spark** in your life?

Fan the Flame
Spend time each day intentionally asking God to help you apply what you've learned in this lesson. Refer to the prayer tips at the beginning of this workbook to provide a framework for your prayer time if you don't already have one. Cultivating a strong prayer life helps you engage the power of the Holy Spirit!

Talk Notes:

"When they heard this, they had no further objections and praised God, saying, 'So then, even to Gentiles God has granted repentance that leads to life.'" Acts 11:18 (NIV)

Lesson 13: Advancements and Adversity Intertwined

Introduction:

As the early church grew and spread, it also faced ongoing adversity. The Jewish leaders continued to antagonize the apostles and believers, hoping to squelch this "Jesus movement." However, they didn't understand the incredible gift of God's Holy Spirit living inside of these men and women. They didn't grasp how He filled believers with supernatural courage, emboldening them to preach the Gospel message despite the threats on their very lives.

1. **The church in Antioch grew as a result of those who fled Jerusalem because of persecution. What do you learn about this church from Acts 11:19-30?**

> "In the midst of the growth of the church in Antioch, followers of Christ — Jews and Gentiles — were first called Christians… The reason is not exactly clear, but some scholars believe 'Christian' was at first a derogatory term; a nickname of sorts…The word is only used three times in the New Testament, each time with a derisive connotation (Acts 11:26; 26:28; 1 Peter 4:16). What likely began as a derogatory term was embraced as early as the second century as a term of endearment then and today for those who follow Jesus of Nazareth."
>
> David Jeremiah[15]

Note: Persecution also spread during this time. King Herod arrested James and some of the other believers. When he realized that by killing James, he grew in popularity with the people, he proceeded to arrest Peter as well, but God had other plans. The night before Peter's trial, he was awakened by an angel and told to get dressed and follow him out of the prison. Peter thought he was dreaming (How many nights had he dreamed of such an escape?), but discovered that he was indeed alive and out of prison! The church had gathered at Mary's home while Peter was in prison, earnestly praying to God for him, and they were astonished when he arrived on their doorstep! Herod killed the guards whose responsibility it had been to keep watch over Peter. Herod eventually experienced a horrific, painful death himself because he did not correct the people when they shouted that he had the voice of a god. Acts 12:5 tells us, "Immediately, because Herod did not give praise to God, an angel of the Lord struck him down, and he was eaten by worms and died." Notice the order of that description. In fact, according to Josephus, a Jewish historian, Herod suffered five days of excruciating pain before his death! Despite the persecution, God's Word continued to spread and flourish! Let's resume our study in Acts 13.

2. How did God's Holy Spirit guide the believers in Antioch in Acts 13:1-5, and how did they respond?

3. Describe the two men who Barnabas and Saul met in Acts 13:6-8.

4. How was Saul (now called Paul) able to discern that the attendant was evil? (Acts 13:9)

5. What do you learn about false teachers / prophets from Matthew 7:15-23?

6. What do you learn about false teachers / prophets from 2 Peter 2?

> "Nothing is more wicked than for someone to claim to speak for God to the salvation of souls when in reality he speaks for Satan to the damnation of souls."
>
> — John MacArthur[16]

7. What warnings are we given about false teachers and false prophets in the following verses:

   • 1 Timothy 4:1-3

   • 2 John 7-11 *(Note: There is only one chapter in 2 John, so this reference is to vereses 7 through 11 in that chapter.)*

8. How should leaders protect their people with regard to false prophets?
   (Acts 20:28-31; 1 Timothy 4:6-8)

9. Focusing again on Paul's confrontation with Elymas in Acts 13:10-12, what punishment did he give the magician for his evil plans, and what ironies do you see in this?

> "The Holy Spirit led Paul to confront Bar-Jesus with his sin. There is a time to be nice and a time to confront. Ask God to show you the difference and to give you the courage to do what is right."
>
> — Life Application Study Bible[17]

10. What happened to the proconsul and why?

Note: Paul, Barnabas, and their companions moved on to Pisidian Antioch where they entered the synagogue on the Sabbath. Paul was given an opportunity to speak publicly so, beginning in the Old Testament, he recounted God's promises and faithful actions to protect and provide for His people. He then recounted the Jewish leadership and followed the lineage of David to the promised Savior, Jesus Christ. Paul continued by saying that the people of Jerusalem and their rulers did not recognize Jesus and condemned Him to die, which resulted in the fulfillment of the same prophecies that were read each Sabbath. After all this, Paul switched the storyline with just two words: BUT GOD. God raised Jesus from the grave, and many witnesses saw Him. This is where we'll resume our study.

11. What is the "good news" that Paul gave in Acts 13:32-33?

12. What role does the Holy Spirit play in this adoption? (Romans 8:12-17)

13. Those in the synagogue initially responded by wanting to hear more, and they invited Paul and Barnabas to return the following Sabbath. Amazingly, almost the entire town gathered on the next Sabbath to hear the Word of the Lord! How did the Jews respond in Acts 13:45?

14. What did Paul and Barnabas say in response, and how did the Gentiles respond to them? (Acts 13:46-48)

15. When the Jewish leaders expelled Paul and Barnabas, what did they do and why? (Acts 13:50-51; Mark 6:7-11)

> "Often Jews would shake the dust off their feet when leaving a Gentile town, on the way back to their own land. This symbolized cleansing themselves from the contamination of those who did not worship God. For Paul and Barnabas to do this to Jews demonstrated that Jews who reject the gospel are not truly part of Israel and are no better than pagans."
>
> Life Application Study Bible[18]

16. How was it possible for the disciples to be filled with joy after they'd been abused, threatened, persecuted, and expelled? How can you apply this in your own life? (Acts 13:52)

 **Pyro Principles:**
What principles did you learn in this week's lesson? Remember, a principle is a truth about God (His person, character, etc.), a promise or warning from God, or a statement of how He relates to mankind.

 *Are you fired up?*
What changes did this week's lesson **spark** in your life?

 Fan the Flame
Spend time each day intentionally asking God to help you apply what you've learned in this lesson. Refer to the prayer tips at the beginning of this workbook to provide a framework for your prayer time if you don't already have one. Cultivating a strong prayer life helps you engage the power of the Holy Spirit!

 *Talk Notes:*

 "The Spirit himself testifies with our spirit that we are God's children. Now if we are children, then we are heirs — heirs of God and co-heirs with Christ, if indeed we share in his sufferings in order that we may also share in his glory."
Romans 8:16-17 (NIV)

Lesson 14: Born Again

Introduction:

We've spent the last several weeks looking at the work of the Holy Spirit in the apostles and the early church. Beginning this week, we will start a series of lessons that will address common phrases about the Holy Spirit that you may have heard used in Christian circles. We will start with the phrase "born again."

Have you ever wondered the origin and meaning of that phrase? Well, you aren't alone! A man named Nicodemus once asked Jesus how a man could be "born again." Let's take a look at his story and what the Bible says about the regenerative work of the Holy Spirit.

1. **Why does mankind need to be born again? (Romans 3:9-20, 23; Ephesians 2:1-3)**

   "No amount of self-improvement or wishful thinking can change man's basic nature. Only God — the One who created us — can re-create us. And that's precisely what He does when we give ourselves to Jesus Christ."

   Billy Graham[19]

2. **What do you learn about Nicodemus from John 3:1-2?**

3. **Why weren't Nicodemus' good works and religious lifestyle enough to be saved at that time, and how does that apply today? (John 3:3; Isaiah 64:6)**

   "Nicodemus had a major flaw in his theology: to him, Jesus was a teacher come from God, not God come to teach. He did not understand that Jesus was God Himself in a body rather than just a representative of God."

   David Jeremiah[20]

4. **According to Jesus' response in John 3:5, what two things are required for someone to enter the kingdom of God and what might He have meant by this?** *(Note: There are various interpretations of this.)*

5. **According to Titus 3:3-7, all three members of the Holy Trinity participate in a believer's salvation. What role does each play?**

6. **The Greek term for "regeneration" ("palingenesias") is only used twice in the entire Bible (Titus 3:5 and Matthew 19:28). Using these two passages, describe the meaning behind the term "regeneration."** (see also Romans 8:22-23)

7. **What do you learn about the Holy Spirit's involvement in regeneration based on the comparison Jesus made between the Spirit and the wind in John 3:8?**

8. **How did the Apostle John describe the "second birth" in John 1:12-13?**

> "Regeneration is not a process, although there may be events, circumstances, witness, influences, and other things that precede it. In other words, there may be many factors and circumstances that lead to a person's conversion, but the actual event of being born again happens instantaneously."
>
> — Charles Ryrie[21]

9. **How did the Apostle Peter describe the "second birth" in 1 Peter 1:23?**

10. How does Romans 6:1-14 describe the rebirth of a believer?

11. Have you been regenerated by the power of the Holy Spirit? If so, briefly share what memories you have of this instantaneous event. Note: If you have not been regenerated by the power of the Holy Spirit, or if you aren't sure, talk with your leader today about what this means and how you can know for sure that you have been saved by faith in Jesus Christ.

12. According to the following Scriptures, what are some of the benefits of being "born again?"

    • Romans 5:1-2

    • 2 Corinthians 5:17

    • Galatians 3:23-25

    • Galatians 3:26

13. Which of these benefits (listed in question #12) excites you the most about your rebirth and why?

> "One may put it all together this way. God regenerates (John 1:13) according to His will (James 1:18) through the sovereign work of the Holy Spirit (John 3:5) when a person believes (John 1:12) the gospel as revealed in the Word of God (1 Peter 1:23)."
>
> — Charles Ryrie[22]

Pyro Principles:
What principles did you learn in this week's lesson? Remember, a principle is a truth about God (His person, character, etc.), a promise or warning from God, or a statement of how He relates to mankind.

Are you fired up?
What changes did this week's lesson **spark** in your life?

Fan the Flame
Spend time each day intentionally asking God to help you apply what you've learned in this lesson. Refer to the prayer tips at the beginning of this workbook to provide a framework for your prayer time if you don't already have one. Cultivating a strong prayer life helps you engage the power of the Holy Spirit!

Talk Notes:

"Therefore, if anyone is in Christ, the new creation has come: The old has gone, the new is here!"
2 Corinthians 5:17 (NIV)

Lesson 15: Illumination of the Spirit

Introduction:

According to the Merriam-Webster Dictionary, the word "illumination" means "the action of spiritual or intellectual enlightenment." Unfortunately, this word has been misused at times, giving it an almost mystical overtone. At the core of this concept, however, is the word "illuminate" which means to shine light on something—that is exactly what the Holy Spirit does! He shines His light on God's Word and on Jesus.

1. Why does mankind need illuminating? (1 Corinthians 2:14; 2 Corinthians 4:3-4)

> "When we talk about spiritual illumination, we are not talking about dreams, special messages, or 'words of knowledge.' What we're talking about is God's Word coming alive to us as the Spirit of God opens our understanding and applies the living Word of God to our own hearts…He [God's Spirit] will never contradict the written Word of God."
>
> — David Jeremiah[23]

2. Give some examples of how you see this in today's culture.

3. In 1 Corinthians 2:6-8, Paul contrasts two different types of wisdom. How are they described and who has each?

4. **The Bible is full of instructions on the importance of God's wisdom and how we can attain it. What do you learn about wisdom from these verses:**

   • **Proverbs 2:1-6**

   • **Proverbs 2:9**

   • **Proverbs 2:10-12, 16**

   • **Proverbs 3:13-15**

   • **James 1:5**

   • **Ephesians 5:15-17; Psalm 90:12**

5. **According to the following verses, how does God reveal His wisdom to us? (John 14:26; 16:12-15; 1 Corinthians 2:10-12)**

> "It is hard to find words in the language of men, to explain the deep things of God. Indeed, there are none that will adequately express what the Spirit of God works in His children. But…by the testimony of the Spirit, I mean, an inward impression on the soul, whereby the Spirit of God immediately and directly witnesses to my spirit, that I am a child of God; that Jesus Christ hath loved me, and given Himself for me; that all my sins are blotted out, and I, even I, am reconciled to God."
>
> — John Wesley[24]

6. **What do you learn in 1 John 2:27a about the "anointing" that believers receive?**

7. **What does John mean when he said "you do not need that anyone teach you" in 1 John 2:27b? What does he NOT mean?**

8. How do we grow in spiritual wisdom and how does the Holy Spirit facilitate this process? (Psalm 1:1-2; Proverbs 2:1-12; John 14:26)

9. In what ways are you intentionally doing this?

> *"Put the Word of God into your heart. Expose yourself to truth… Fill your spiritual computer with truth and in the moment when you need it, the Holy Spirit will cause you to remember the things you've learned. In computer terms, He is the 'Search Engine' who locates exactly what you need. It's His ministry. It's His Specialty. It's His delight."*
>
> — David Jeremiah[25]

10. In Ephesians 3:1-7, what "mystery" does Paul describe?

11. How was this mystery revealed and what does that tell you about the Holy Spirit's illuminating activities? (Ephesians 3:5; Acts 10:27-28; 11:15-18)

12. In what area of your life do you need the Spirit's wisdom and illumination right now?

13. Specifically, what changes will you make in your life this week to enable that to happen (within God's will and timing)?

 **Pyro Principles:**
What principles did you learn in this week's lesson? Remember, a principle is a truth about God (His person, character, etc.), a promise or warning from God, or a statement of how He relates to mankind.

 *Are you fired up?*
What changes did this week's lesson **spark** in your life?

 Fan the Flame
Spend time each day intentionally asking God to help you apply what you've learned in this lesson. Refer to the prayer tips at the beginning of this workbook to provide a framework for your prayer time if you don't already have one. Cultivating a strong prayer life helps you engage the power of the Holy Spirit!

 *Talk Notes:*

 "Blessed is the one who does not walk in step with the wicked or stand in the way that sinners take or sit in the company of mockers, but whose delight is in the law of the Lord, and who meditates on his law day and night." Psalm 1:1-2 (NIV)

Lesson 16: Muddy Waters: Baptism by the Holy Spirit

Introduction:

The term "baptism by the Holy Spirit" is often misunderstood, causing confusion and sometimes division among believers. The purpose of this week's lesson is not to attack any single group of people or beliefs, but rather to search the Bible for what God has said about baptism by His Spirit.

Note that there is a distinction between being **baptized** by the Spirit and being **filled** with the Spirit (which we will study in greater depth next week). Sometimes these two terms are mistakenly used interchangeably, but they are not synonymous terms.

Before you begin this lesson, ask the Holy Spirit to help you set aside any previous ideas or beliefs you may have about this topic and attempt to study what the Bible says about it without prejudice. What you or I say is true doesn't matter — **what matters is what GOD has said is true in His Word.**

1. **The concept of "baptism" is used in many contexts in the Bible. Look up the following verses and describe the concept in each passage. The first one has been done for you as an example —**

    • **Matthew 15:2; Mark 7:3-4** — *Jewish ceremonial practice of washing / cleansing / purifying of hands, utensils, etc. with water.*

    • **Matthew 3:5-6,11a; Acts 19:4** (often called "John's baptism")

    • **Mark 10:38-39**

    • **John 9:7-15; 13:5-14**

2. How is baptism described in Ephesians 4:5?

> "The baptism of the Spirit did something God had never done before in history. It united believers with Christ in a new relationship: as fellow members of the spiritual body of Christ (John 14:17: 'He abides with you and will be in you.'). Believers then shared the life of Christ in a way never before experienced. God united them with Him. The same Spirit of God that indwelled Him now indwells us."
>
> — Dr. Thomas L. Constable[26]

3. Describe the baptism referred to in 1 Corinthians 12:13? What was / is the purpose of this baptism?

4. What contrast did John the Baptist make in Matthew 3:11 that Jesus repeated in Acts 1:5?

5. Why was Jesus, who was without sin (2 Corinthians 5:21a), baptized by John? (Matthew 3:13-17)

6. **Christians have been divided for many years over the timing of the baptism of the Holy Spirit. Some denominations believe that it happens simultaneously with the "second birth" that we discussed last week. Other denominations hold to the belief that the baptism of the Holy Spirit is something that comes later and should be sought. There are a couple of examples of conversions with a delayed onset of the Holy Spirit in the early church that are used in this debate…let's examine them:**

   <u>*The Gospel Spreads to the Samaritans (Acts 8:1-25)*</u>

   • **Summarize Philip's activities and how the people responded (8:5-8, 12-13)**

   • **What was the "spiritual status" of these people prior to Peter and John's visit? (8:14-16)**

   > *"You should not expect the baptism of the Holy Spirit except at the moment of salvation. There isn't one command in all of the New Testament to seek for the baptism of the Holy Spirit. Why would there be? It isn't something you seek for. It's something that God does for you. There isn't one instruction in Scripture on how to get the baptism of the Holy Spirit. Though you search the New Testament from beginning to end, you'll never find it. You don't need to be instructed on how to get something that has been done for you."*
   >
   > — David Jeremiah[27]

   • **What did Peter and John do? (8:14-17)**

The Gospel Spreads to Ephesus (Acts 18:24-19:7)

• **Who was Apollos and what did he know and not know? (18:24-25)**

• **How does that background affect your understanding of Paul's question in Acts 19:1-2?**

• **What happened to these twelve men when they were baptized in the name of the Lord Jesus and Paul laid his hands on them? (19:5-7)**

• **What purpose would the gift of tongues serve as these transformed disciples returned to be among their people?**

7. **Do the examples given in question #6 teach that there is a <u>DELAY</u> in receiving the Holy Spirit after placing faith in Jesus? Why or why not?**

> *"To summarize, it is my belief that Pentecost instituted the Church. Then all that remained was for Samaritans, Gentiles, and 'belated believers' to be brought into the Church representatively. This occurred in Acts 8 for Samaritans, Acts 10 for Gentiles (according to Acts 11:15), and Acts 19 for 'belated believers' from John's baptism. Once this representative baptism with the Spirit occurred, the normal pattern applied — baptism with the Spirit at the time each person (of whatever background) believed in Jesus Christ."*
>
> — Billy Graham[28]

8. **Summarize what you've learned about the baptism of the Holy Spirit this week.**

 **Pyro Principles:**
What principles did you learn in this week's lesson? Remember, a principle is a truth about God (His person, character, etc.), a promise or warning from God, or a statement of how He relates to mankind.

 *Are you fired up?*
What changes did this week's lesson **spark** in your life?

 **Fan the Flame**
Spend time each day intentionally asking God to help you apply what you've learned in this lesson. Refer to the prayer tips at the beginning of this workbook to provide a framework for your prayer time if you don't already have one. Cultivating a strong prayer life helps you engage the power of the Holy Spirit!

 Talk Notes:

 "I baptize you with water for repentance. But after me comes one who is more powerful than I, whose sandals I am not worthy to carry. He will baptize you with the Holy Spirit and fire." Matthew 3:11 (NIV)

Lesson 17: Sealed by the Holy Spirit

Introduction:

Last week, we talked about the baptism of the Spirit. This week, we'll study what it means to be sealed by the Holy Spirit. Merriam-Webster defines the word "seal" as "something that confirms, ratifies, or makes secure; a guarantee; assurance." Let's look at the use of the term "seal" in a broader sense as well as the specific sealing by the Holy Spirit.

1. **According to 2 Corinthians 1:21-22, Who seals believers by the Holy Spirit?**

2. **According to that same passage, the seal is described as a guarantee. What is it guaranteeing? (2 Corinthians 5:1-5; Ephesians 1:13-14; 4:30; Romans 8:23)**

3. **Describe the audience to whom Paul was writing. (1 Corinthians 1:1-2; 4:18-21; 5:1-8)**

4. What does this tell you about who receives the seal of the Holy Spirit? Is it possible to be redeemed by faith but not sealed by the Holy Spirit?

5. When are believers sealed by the Holy Spirit? (Ephesians 1:13)

6. What is promised (either directly or indirectly) with the seal? (Ephesians 1:13; Romans 8:14-17)

> "Perhaps best of all, the presence of the Holy Spirit, living in fellowship with us, provides us with a foretaste, a sample, of our coming life and inheritance in God's presence."
>
> Billy Graham[29]

7. What is NOT promised with the seal? (John 15:18-21; James 1:2-4)

8. How do the following uses of the word or concept behind "seal" in the Bible provide additional insight into the seal of the Holy Spirit?

- Esther 8:8

- Jeremiah 32:9-10

- Daniel 6:17; Matthew 27:62-66

9. How do the tangible illustrations of a seal and earnest money / deposit (as given in Ephesians 1:13-14) affect your view of being sealed by God's Spirit?

10. What encouragement and comfort do you draw from what you've learned in this week's lesson?

> *"The allusion to the seal as the proof of purchase would have been especially significant to the Ephesians. The city of Ephesus was a seaport, and the shipmasters of the neighboring ports carried on an extensive trade in timber. The method of purchase was this: the merchant, after selecting his timber, stamped it with his own signet — an acknowledged sign of ownership. In due time the merchant would send a trusted agent with the signet; he would locate all the timbers that bore the corresponding impress and claim them."*
>
> Billy Graham[30]

 **Pyro Principles:**
What principles did you learn in this week's lesson? Remember, a principle is a truth about God (His person, character, etc.), a promise or warning from God, or a statement of how He relates to mankind.

 *Are you fired up?*
What changes did this week's lesson **spark** in your life?

 **Fan the Flame**
Spend time each day intentionally asking God to help you apply what you've learned in this lesson. Refer to the prayer tips at the beginning of this workbook to provide a framework for your prayer time if you don't already have one. Cultivating a strong prayer life helps you engage the power of the Holy Spirit!

 Talk Notes:

 "Now it is God who makes both us and you stand firm in Christ. He anointed us, set his seal of ownership on us, and put his Spirit in our hearts as a deposit, guaranteeing what is to come." 2 Corinthians 1:21-22 (NIV)

Lesson 18: Filled with the Holy Spirit

Introduction:

In contrast to baptism by the Spirit, which happens only once (when you place your faith in Jesus) and cannot be undone, being filled with the Spirit is an ongoing process and can be lost. It's like a bucket with holes punched all around it — the more you fill it, the more will flow out of it. You have to consistently pour water into it in order to have water consistently flow out of it. The same is true for our Christian walk. The more we are filled with the Spirit, the more He flows through us to others. But we have to consistently be **refilled** with Him.

A Spirit-filled life requires obedience and submission. We must give up control of our life, sacrificing our will for God's will. This allows God to fill us with His Holy Spirit who will gradually invade every area of our life and transform us for God's glory and the benefit of others!

1. **What worldly or secular things "fill" you on occasion? …fear? …greed and ambition? …anger? …lust? …something else?**

2. **In Ephesians 5:15-18, Paul gave several instructions for how to live a life filled by the Spirit. List some of these dos and don'ts.**

> "Many people will take notes on a sermon and promptly file them in the back of their Bible. They won't really think very much about the message after that, because the general mentality in the evangelical world goes something like this: We don't want to be lost, but we don't want to be so Spirit-filled that we can't enjoy the mediocrity of a middle-of-the-road position."
>
> David Jeremiah[31]

3. **The command to be filled with the Spirit is given in the passive voice which means the filling is not something we can do for ourselves. However, there are steps we can and should take to put ourselves in a better position to receive the filling of God's Holy Spirit. Using the verses below, what are some of these steps?**

   • **Psalm 42:1-2; Matthew 5:6; John 7:37-38**

   • **Psalm 139:23-24; 2 Corinthians 7:1**

   • **Romans 12:1-2**

   • **Psalm 119:9-16**

4. What perspective is described in Ephesians 5:16, and how can you apply that perspective in your own life? (I Peter 1:17)

5. What sin is described in James 4:17 and how does that relate to Ephesians 5:15-17?

6. Describe the comparison made in Ephesians 5:18.

7. According to Ephesians 5:19-21, what are the results of being "filled with the Spirit"?

> "We should not be concerned with how much of the Holy Spirit we have, but how much of us the Holy Spirit has. Submit yourself daily to his leading and draw constantly on his power."
>
> Life Application Study Bible[32]

8. Why did Paul talk about the need to be filled with the Spirit before he gave instructions for submission, honor, respect, and obedience among multiple types of relationships? How can you improve the relationships in your life?

9. Do you know a believer who you would describe as being "filled with the Spirit"? What makes them stand out from others? In what ways to you recognize the Holy Spirit in them? Be sure to send them a quick note of encouragement this week saying that you've noticed the Spirit at work in and through them and to keep it up!

10. Does every believer experience being "filled with the Spirit"? (Acts 6:3)

11. Why do you think some believers don't WANT to be "filled with the Spirit"? What truth are they missing? (2 Corinthians 3:7-18)

12. What about you? Do you honestly WANT to be "filled with the Spirit"? Is anything holding you back from allowing God free reign in your life? Is there an area of your life that you are unwilling to surrender to God?

 **Pyro Principles:**
What principles did you learn in this week's lesson? Remember, a principle is a truth about God (His person, character, etc.), a promise or warning from God, or a statement of how He relates to mankind.

 *Are you fired up?*
What changes did this week's lesson **spark** in your life?

 **Fan the Flame**
Spend time each day intentionally asking God to help you apply what you've learned in this lesson. Refer to the prayer tips at the beginning of this workbook to provide a framework for your prayer time if you don't already have one. Cultivating a strong prayer life helps you engage the power of the Holy Spirit!

 Talk Notes:

 "May the God of hope fill you with all joy and peace as you trust in him, so that you may overflow with hope by the power of the Holy Spirit." Romans 15:13 (NIV)

Lesson 19: Walking with the Holy Spirit

Introduction:

A popular term in the Christian world is to refer to the believers' "walk with God." In contrast to being "filled with the Spirit" as we studied last week, "walking with the Spirit" focuses on the DOING rather than the BEING. Just like the verb "walk" implies action, so does our walk with the Spirit.

1. How would you currently describe your walk with God? Is it a meandering stroll? Is it a power walk or are you stumbling along? Use a Thesaurus to look up some alternative words for "walk" and see which one fits your spiritual journey best.

2. Look up each of the following verses to discover how the Bible describes the "Christian walk" (hint: you may want to use the NKJV or the ESV to see the use of the word "walk").

   • Romans 13:13

   • 2 Corinthians 5:7

   • Ephesians 2:10

   • Ephesians 5:2

   • Ephesians 5:8-14

   • Colossians 1:10

   • 1 John 2:6

> "Spiritual Power is not necessarily or usually the miraculous or spectacular, but rather the consistent exhibition of the characteristics of the Lord Jesus in the believer's life."
>
> — Charles Ryrie[33]

3. What does Paul mean by what he said in Galatians 5:18? (Gal 5:3-6)

4. What does a life "led by the flesh" look like and what are the consequences of such a lifestyle? (Gal. 5:19-21)

5. Does this mean that someone who claims to be a Christian but struggles with one or more of these sins isn't a believer? (Romans 7:14-25; 1 John 3:9)

6. Describe the relationship between the Spirit and the flesh. (Galatians 5:16-18; Ephesians 6:10-12)

> "The solution to the flesh is not found in fighting the flesh, but in welcoming the Spirit."
>
> Cultural Backgrounds Study Bible[34]

7. What steps can you take to engage in this spiritual battle? (Ephesians 6:10-11, 13-20; 2 Corinthians 10:3-5)

8. What difference does prayer make in this battle? (Ephesians 6:18-20; 2 Corinthians 1:8-11)

9. According to Paul's example in Ephesians 3:14-19, how should we pray for fellow believers, and what role does the Holy Spirit play in this process?

10. When believers stand firm against the devil, what are some positive effects for the entire body of believers worldwide? (Philippians 1:12-14; 1 Thessalonians 1:2-10; 3:1-10; 1 Peter 5:8-9)

11. What changes will you make in your prayer life as a result of this lesson and how will it affect your walk with the Holy Spirit?

> "Satan, the real adversary, has a way of getting people to blame each other or God for their sufferings. To help his readers keep the blame where it belongs, Peter writes that Satan is like a half-starved lion in his restless hunger to find, defeat, and devour God's children, especially in times of suffering. Although no one should ever underestimate the devil, God is greater. So when Christians resist Satan in the power of the Holy Spirit, the enemy flees (Ephesians 6:12-18; James 4:7)."
>
> David Jeremiah[35]

 **Pyro Principles:**
What principles did you learn in this week's lesson? Remember, a principle is a truth about God (His person, character, etc.), a promise or warning from God, or a statement of how He relates to mankind.

 *Are you fired up?*
What changes did this week's lesson **spark** in your life?

 Fan the Flame
Spend time each day intentionally asking God to help you apply what you've learned in this lesson. Refer to the prayer tips at the beginning of this workbook to provide a framework for your prayer time if you don't already have one. Cultivating a strong prayer life helps you engage the power of the Holy Spirit!

 Talk Notes:

"So I say, walk by the Spirit, and you will not gratify the desires of the flesh." Galatians 5:16 (NIV)

Lesson 20: Where There's Smoke, There's Fire: Spiritual Fruit

Introduction:

When a believer is walking with the Spirit, the fruit of the Spirit will be evident in his or her life. But what does that look like? What is the "fruit" and how do we cultivate it? Let's discover what God has to say about this topic and then apply what we learn to improve our "walk" with the Spirit.

1. **Fill in the chart below with the nine characteristics that are indicative of a life "led by the Spirit" (Gal 5:22-26). Then describe in greater detail each of these characteristics using the following verses — the first one has been done as an example for you.**

Characteristic	Verses to look up	Describe in greater detail
Love	Matthew 22:34-40; John 13:35; 1 Corinthians 13:4-8a, 13	Our most important command is to love God and love others — all the law depends on these two rules. Love is patient, kind, trusting, humble, & selfless. It keeps no record of wrongs and finds no joy in unrighteousness but rejoices in the truth. It bears, believes, hopes, and endures all things. It never fails and never ends. Our love for one another demonstrates our love for Jesus.
	James 1:2-3; Nehemiah 8:10	
	John 16:33; Philippians 4:6-7	

Characteristic	Verses to look up	Describe in greater detail
	Ephesians 4:1-3; James 5:7-11	
	Ephesians 2:4-10; 4:32	
	Galatians 6:9-10	
	Revelation 2:10b	
	Galatians 6:1	
	Titus 2:11-12	

2. **Which item on the list of spiritual fruit do you struggle with the most? Which one is the easiest for you to live?**

3. **What encourages the growth of spiritual fruit in a believer's life? (Psalm 1:1-3; John 15:1-11)**

> "The word for 'peace' in the Greek language is the word 'iranai' [or 'eirene'] and it means 'to join together.' It is a picture of two opposing forces once separated but now reconciled. Do you know what peace is? Peace is knowing that the God you were once separated from, you are now joined to through Jesus Christ."
>
> David Jeremiah[36]

4. **What results from a life that bears abundant spiritual fruit? (John 15:8)**

5. **How did Jesus exemplify these nine characteristics of spiritual fruit in His life and how can you apply this in your own life as you follow Him?**

   • Love (John 15:9-17)

   • Joy (Luke 10:21)

   • Peace (John 14:27)

> "Sadly, the virtue of kindness is becoming more and more unusual in our world. What were once 'common courtesies' are becoming most uncommon. We live in an angry world. A world with a chip on its shoulder. A world that's in a big hurry…We're living in an era that is forgetting what it means to be kind, and people get run over by other people in a hurry to meet their own goals."
>
> David Jeremiah[37]

- **Patience (1 Timothy 1:15-17)**

- **Kindness (Ephesians 2:6-7)**

- **Goodness (John 10:1-18)**

- **Faithfulness (Hebrews 3:6)**

- **Gentleness (Matthew 11:28-30; 21:5)**

- **Self-Control (1 Peter 2:23)**

6. How are "faith" and "fruit" interrelated? (2 Peter 1:3-11)

7. How does spiritual fruit help you fulfill Jesus' two greatest commandments found in Matthew 22:34-40? (1 Corinthians 13:4-7)

8. **How does spiritual fruit help you recognize people who want to mislead you and direct you away from God? (Matthew 7:15-23)**

> "Without the vine, the branch can do nothing. So it is with our lives. As long as I strain and work to produce the fruit of the Spirit from within myself, I will end up fruitless and frustrated. But as I abide in Christ — as I maintain a close, obedient, dependent relationship with Him — God the Holy Spirit works in my life, creating in me the fruit of the Spirit. That does not mean we instantly become mature, bearing all the fruit of the Spirit fully and immediately. The fruit on fruit trees takes time to mature, and pruning may be necessary before fruit is produced in quantity. So it may be with us."
>
> — Billy Graham[38]

9. **What tangible changes will you make in your life this week to cultivate a life that is fruitbearing through the power of the Holy Spirit?**

 **Pyro Principles:**
What principles did you learn in this week's lesson? Remember, a principle is a truth about God (His person, character, etc.), a promise or warning from God, or a statement of how He relates to mankind.

 **Are you fired up?**
What changes did this week's lesson **spark** in your life?

 Fan the Flame
Spend time each day intentionally asking God to help you apply what you've learned in this lesson. Refer to the prayer tips at the beginning of this workbook to provide a framework for your prayer time if you don't already have one. Cultivating a strong prayer life helps you engage the power of the Holy Spirit!

 **Talk Notes:**

 "I am the vine; you are the branches. If you remain in me and I in you, you will bear much fruit; apart from me, you can do nothing." John 15:5 (NIV)

Lesson 21: Where There's Smoke, There's Fire: Spiritual Gifts

Introduction:

When a believer is walking with the Spirit, not only will the fruit of the Spirit be evident in his or her life, but also the gifts of the Spirit will equip the believer to supernaturally fulfill God's will. This week, we will address common questions regarding spiritual gifts, and next week, we will further examine the category of spiritual gifts generally referred to as the "sign" gifts.

1. **Before we study the gifts themselves, let's establish a general background. What are some purposes of spiritual gifts? (Ephesians 4:12,16; 1 Corinthians 12:7; 1 Peter 4:10-11)**

2. **Who receives gifts from the Spirit? (1 Corinthians 12:7; 1 Peter 4:10)**

3. **Who determines our spiritual gifts? (1 Corinthians 12:11)**

4. **As described in 2 Timothy 1:6-7, what can sometimes prevent us from fully using our spiritual gifts and how does God help us overcome it?**

Did you know?

The word translated as "gift" in the passages traditionally used in reference to spiritual gifts is the same word used in Romans 1:11 where Paul says he longs to see the believers in Rome so that he may "impart" to them some "spiritual gift." However, we know that all spiritual gifts are given by God, not by man, so what might this mean? According to David Jeremiah[39], the word 'gift' in Romans 1:11 "is used in the general sense of 'blessing,' probably referring to Paul's preaching." Our gifts, when used correctly, are a blessing to others!

5. **What spiritual gifts are listed in each of the following passages?**

   • **Romans 12:6-8**

   • **1 Corinthians 12:8-10, 28**

   • **Ephesians 4:11**

6. **How does Paul describe the church body using the illustration of the physical body in 1 Corinthians 12:12-19?**

> *"Having a spiritual gift doesn't mean you are 'spiritual.' Far from it. The fact is, most of the truth about spiritual gifts is recorded in Paul's first letter to the Church at Corinth…easily the most carnal church in the whole New Testament! The Bible says of this church that they came short in no gift (1 Corinthians 1:7). The Corinthian church had 'em all! Yet they were tragically, embarrassingly immature and carnal."*
>
> — Dr. David Jeremiah[40]

7. **Describe the beautiful design God has for the functionality of the church body. (1 Corinthians 12:20-26)**

8. **What does Paul mean by his instruction to "earnestly desire the greater gifts" in 1 Corinthians 12:31? What does he NOT mean?**

9. **What does Paul mean by his comment at the end of 1 Corinthians 12:31, "And yet I will show you the most excellent way"?**

10. **What are the general themes of 1 Corinthians chapters 12, 13, and 14, and why do you think chapter 13 is inserted in the middle of what otherwise seems like an ongoing topic?**

11. **As previously discussed, spiritual gifts are not for the benefit of the believer exercising the gift but for the benefit of the church and fellow believers. However, what the believer does with his or her gift has future rewards and / or judgment. Describe these rewards and judgments based on the following verses: 1 Corinthians 3:10-15; 2 Corinthians 5:9-10.**

12. **Some spiritual gifts are also instructions given to ALL believers. For example, Billy Graham clearly had the spiritual gift of evangelism. He was uniquely created to be able to tell others about Jesus in such a powerful way that millions were impacted for eternity. However, ALL believers are instructed to tell others about the gospel of Jesus Christ (Acts 1:8), even if they don't have the gift of evangelism. What other spiritual gifts from the lists in question 4 are also required of ALL believers? (Matthew 28:20; 2 Corinthians 5:7; 9:7; Galatians 5:13; Hebrews 3:13; Hebrews 10:25; James 1:5; 2 Peter 3:18; 1 John 4:1)**

13. **Do you know your spiritual gift(s)? If so, share how you are currently using your gift(s) for the glory of God and the benefit of other believers.** *Note: If you don't know your spiritual gift(s), check this week's "Next Step News" for a free gifts assessment you can take.*

> "Spiritual gifts should not be sought as ends in themselves. In some circles, there is a tendency to exalt the gifts above the Giver."
>
> — Dr. Kenneth Boa[41]

 **Pyro Principles:**
What principles did you learn in this week's lesson? Remember, a principle is a truth about God (His person, character, etc.), a promise or warning from God, or a statement of how He relates to mankind.

 **Are you fired up?**
What changes did this week's lesson **spark** in your life?

 Fan the Flame
Spend time each day intentionally asking God to help you apply what you've learned in this lesson. Refer to the prayer tips at the beginning of this workbook to provide a framework for your prayer time if you don't already have one. Cultivating a strong prayer life helps you engage the power of the Holy Spirit!

 Talk Notes:

"For we are God's handiwork, created in Christ Jesus to do good works, which God prepared in advance for us to do." Eph 2:10 (NIV)

Lesson 22: Looking for a Sign

Introduction:

Last week, we laid a solid foundation in our understanding of spiritual gifts. Now, let's build on that foundation as we further examine the gifts that are often the source of controversy and division among believers: the "sign" gifts which traditionally consist of healings, miracles, tongues, and interpretation of tongues.

This is a complicated topic that dates all the way back to the Council of Nicaea in AD 325. Numerous books and articles have been written about the sign gifts (some of which we recommend in this week's "Next Step News" for further study if you are interested). Obviously, we won't be able to cover this hot topic exhaustively in one lesson, so in the interest of time, here is a framework that describes the four primary positions taken within the evangelical movement as defined by Wayne Grudem in the book, "Are Miraculous Gifts for Today?"[42] —

1) Cessationist — This position "argues that there are no miraculous gifts of the Holy Spirit today. Gifts such as prophecy, tongues, and healing were confined to the first century, and were used at the time the apostles were establishing the churches and the New Testament was not yet complete. This is a well-defined and often-defended position within evangelical scholarship."

2) Pentecostal / Charismatic — The **pentecostal** position "refers to any denomination or group that traces its historical origin back to the Pentecostal revival that began in the United States in 1901, and that holds the following doctrines: 1) All the gifts of the Holy Spirit mentioned in the New Testament are intended for today; 2) baptism in the Holy Spirit is an empowering experience subsequent to conversion and should be sought by Christians today; and 3) when baptism in the Holy Spirit occurs, people will speak in tongues as a "sign" that they have received this experience. Pentecostal groups usually have their own distinct denominational structures, among which are the Assemblies of God, the Church of God in Christ, and many others." The **charismatic** position "refers to any groups (or people) that trace their historical origin to the charismatic renewal movement of the 1960s and 1970s and that seek to practice all the spiritual gifts mentioned in the New Testament…Among charismatics, there are differing viewpoints on whether baptism in the Holy Spirit is subsequent to conversion and whether speaking in tongues is a sign of baptism in the Spirit. Charismatics by and large have refrained from forming their own denominations, but view themselves as a force for renewal within existing Protestant and Roman Catholic churches."

3) The Third Wave — This position arose in the 1980s by a missions professor named C. Peter Wagner at Fuller Seminary. "Third Wave people encourage the equipping of all believers to use New Testament spiritual gifts today and say that the proclamation of the gospel should ordinarily be accompanied by 'signs, wonders, and miracles,' according to the New Testament pattern. They teach, however, that baptism in the Holy Spirit happens to all Christians at conversion and that subsequent experiences are better called 'fillings' or 'empowerings' with the Holy Spirit. Though they believe the gift of tongues exists today, they do not emphasize it to the extent that Pentecostals and charismatics do."

4) Open but Cautious — This position is likely held by a large number of evangelicals "who think of themselves as belonging to none of these groups. These people have not been convinced by the cessationist arguments that relegate certain gifts to the first century, but they are not really convinced by the doctrine or practice of those who emphasize such gifts today either. They are open to the possibility of miraculous gifts today, but they are concerned about the possibility of abuses that they have seen in groups that practice these gifts."

With that as a background, let's see what the Bible says about each of the sign gifts.

Healings

1. What do you learn about the Apostle Paul from Acts 19:11-12?

2. With that in mind, what is significant about Paul's advice to Timothy in 1 Timothy 5:23 and Paul's comment about Trophimus in 2 Timothy 4:20?

3. How did God use Paul's pain and suffering in 2 Corinthians 12:7b-10?

4. How does this apply today? (Romans 8:28)

5. **Can you think of an example today or in the recent past of a believer whose suffering produced good for others?**

> "In seeking God's power, I discovered his person. He is not just omnipotent; he is also the God of all comfort. And taking us through suffering, not out of it, is one of the primary means that the Spirit uses today in bringing us to God."
>
> — Daniel B. Wallace[43]

6. **How do some people confuse the gift of healings with the gift of faith, and in what ways are they distinct gifts? (Matthew 17:20)**

7. **What was the purpose of miracles in the early church according to Paul in 2 Corinthians 12:12?**

> "Why do we not see the spectacular miracles today that we read about in the Bible? Are few such miracles occurring because our faith is small — or could it be that God does not will the spectacular right now? Could it be that signs and wonders were gifts particularly appropriate to the special circumstances of the early Church? I think so. And today when the gospel is proclaimed on the frontiers of the Christian faith that approximate the first century situation, miracles still sometimes accompany the advance of the gospel."
>
> — Billy Graham[44]

8. **What do we have now that serves the purpose of authenticating authority that was not available in the early church? (Acts 17:11)**

Tongues and Interpretation of Tongues

9. The primary passages regarding tongues are Acts 2:1-12; 1 Corinthians 12:10b, 28-30; and 1 Corinthians 14:1-28. Compare these descriptions of speaking in tongues and explain the differences you see.

10. Who are tongues a sign for according to 1 Corinthians 14:22-25?

General Questions

11. What problem is sometimes connected to many spiritual gifts, but especially to "sign" gifts and why is this not pleasing to the Lord? (Galatians 6:3)

12. Why do some Christians believe these gifts are still active today and other Christians believe they are dormant?
    Note: you may need to refer to supplemental reading to answer this question. We have provided a few links in this week's "Next Step News" to assist you.

13. **Why must we be very careful to hold to Scripture as having higher authority than personal experiences or the experiences of those we know, particularly if they are in contradiction? (Matthew 7:15; 2 Peter 1:20-21)**

14. **What do you believe about the "sign gifts" and why?**

> "One of the reasons why there is so much controversy today over whether or not you should be using these gifts in the church is simply because men and women haven't sat down with their Bibles to determine why the gift was given in the first place. Why was there a sign gift? When Jesus was preaching, and when the apostles followed Him in the afterglow of His ministry, there was no New Testament as we have it today. How would a person know if the word of this young rabbi from Nazareth was authoritative? The only way they would know that was if His preaching was authenticated in such a way that they could not miss the miraculous nature of His communication. How were the apostles to be identified and authenticated after Christ went back to heaven? It was only because of their sign gifts. The sign gift was a visible demonstration that what they spoke was the Word of God. That was its purpose."
>
> Dr. David Jeremiah[45]

15. **In your opinion, how has the global church body allowed this matter to divide congregations? Do you think this is pleasing to the Lord? (1 Corinthians 1:10-11; 12:24b-25)**

 **Pyro Principles:**
What principles did you learn in this week's lesson? Remember, a principle is a truth about God (His person, character, etc.), a promise or warning from God, or a statement of how He relates to mankind.

 *Are you fired up?*
What changes did this week's lesson **spark** in your life?

 Fan the Flame
Spend time each day intentionally asking God to help you apply what you've learned in this lesson. Refer to the prayer tips at the beginning of this workbook to provide a framework for your prayer time if you don't already have one. Cultivating a strong prayer life helps you engage the power of the Holy Spirit!

 *Talk Notes:*

 "There are different kinds of gifts, but the same Spirit distributes them. There are different kinds of service, but the same Lord. There are different kinds of working, but in all of them and in everyone it is the same God at work." 1 Corinthians 12:4-6 (NIV)

Lesson 23: Viewing Today in Light of the Future

Introduction:

Over the past several months, we've studied the Holy Spirit's presence in specific people and instances in the Old Testament, His presence during the time of Jesus' birth and life, His "debut" in Acts, and how He transformed the early church in such a way that the gospel message of Jesus Christ spread like wildfire!

But what happens next? What's the "rest of the story?" That's actually not as clear as most people would like for it to be because while the Bible talks exhaustively about the end times, the specific involvement of the Holy Spirit is not mentioned very much. We will do our best to consider what we ARE told about the future, with an emphasis on the presence and activities of the Holy Spirit. Then, we'll consider how that future should impact us today.

1. **Where does the Holy Spirit currently reside? (1 Corinthians 3:16; 6:19)**

2. **What happens to believers at the rapture? (1 Thessalonians 4:13-18)**

3. **Based on that information, what conclusions can you draw about the presence of the Holy Spirit on this earth after the rapture? In what ways might His ministry be similar to past times?**

4. **What specific activities of the Holy Spirit are described in the following verses?**

   • John 6:63; Romans 8:9-11; Galatians 6:8

   • Zechariah 12:10; Ezekiel 36:26-27

> "Civilization still has a veneer of decency through law enforcement, education, science, and reason. Although we are horrified by criminal acts, we have yet to see the real horror of complete lawlessness…People totally without God can act no better than vicious animals. Lawlessness, to a certain extent, is already going on, but the man of lawlessness has not yet been revealed."
>
> Life Application Study Bible[46]

5. **In 2 Thessalonians 2, Paul encourages the church to NOT believe the false rumors that were spreading about the rapture having already happened. How does Paul describe the work of the Holy Spirit in verses 6-8a?**

6. **When that happens, what will life on earth look like? (Matthew 24:12, 21-22; 2 Timothy 3:1-9)**

7. **In what ways will Satan have the power to deceive as the Day of the Lord draws near? (Matthew 24:24; 2 Corinthians 11:14-15)**

> "…as we approach the end of the age I believe we will see a dramatic recurrence of signs and wonders that will demonstrate the power of God to a skeptical world. Just as the powers of Satan are being unleashed with greater intensity, so I believe God will allow signs and wonders to be performed."
>
> Billy Graham[47]

8. **Why does this make the complete fulfillment of Joel 2:28-32 necessary at that time? (2 Corinthians 4:4-6; 11:13-15)**

9. Knowing just how horrific the Tribulation period will be, and even worse, how horrific and eternal hell will be, what passion / burden should the body of Christ have in today's age? (John 1:29)

> *"Only God can thwart the plans of Satan and his legions, because only God is all-powerful. Only His Holy Spirit can bring true spiritual awakening that will stem the tide of evil and reverse the trend. In the darkest hour God can still revive His people, and by the Holy Spirit breathe new vigor and power into the body of Christ."*
>
> — Billy Graham[48]

10. The Merriam-Webster Dictionary defines the term to "revive" as "to restore to consciousness or life; to restore from a depressed, inactive, or unused state; to bring back; or to renew in the mind or memory." How would you describe a spiritual revival using that definition?

11. While there is no "magic formula" when it comes to spiritual revival (remember John 3:8), there are some steps we can take to encourage spiritual revival in ourselves, our homes & families, our communities, our churches, and our nation. What are some of these action steps?

    • Revelation 3:17

    • 1 John 1:9

    • Romans 12:1-2

    • Hebrews 12:1-2

12. What specific instructions does Paul give believers in Colossians 4:2-4 and how can you apply them to encourage spiritual revival?

Pyro Principles:
What principles did you learn in this week's lesson? Remember, a principle is a truth about God (His person, character, etc.), a promise or warning from God, or a statement of how He relates to mankind.

Are you fired up?
What changes did this week's lesson **spark** in your life?

Fan the Flame
Spend time each day intentionally asking God to help you apply what you've learned in this lesson. Refer to the prayer tips at the beginning of this workbook to provide a framework for your prayer time if you don't already have one. Cultivating a strong prayer life helps you engage the power of the Holy Spirit!

Talk Notes:

"The wind blows wherever it pleases. You hear its sound, but you cannot tell where it comes from or where it is going. So it is with everyone born of the Spirit." John 3:8 (NIV)

Lesson 24: How Then Shall We Live?

Introduction:

Wow — what a year it's been! There's so much to be learned through the study of God's Word. Let's conclude this study with our final lesson by answering the "so what?" question. How should we live as a result of what we've learned?

1. The book of Jude describes the spiritual battle between good and evil that has raged for centuries and will continue to rage until the day of judgment. As you read through it (*don't worry — it's only one chapter long!*), what do you learn about this spiritual battle and the consequences for those who choose to go against God and pursue the desires of the flesh?

2. What two ungodly activities are described in Jude 4b? Give some examples of how you see that happening in today's society.

3. According to Jude 19, what are the ungodly missing?

> "If you believe in Jesus Christ, a power is available to you that can change your life…unfortunately, this power has been ignored, misunderstood, and misused. By our ignorance we have short-circuited the power of the Holy Spirit."
>
> Billy Graham[49]

4. In the midst of a culture that is sinful, blind, and self-destructive, how should believers live? (Jude 20-23)

5. According to the following verses, what difference does the Holy Spirit make in the life of a believer?

   • Romans 5:5

   • Romans 8:26

   • Romans 9:1

   • Romans 15:13

   • 1 Corinthians 6:19

   • Titus 3:5

   • 2 Timothy 1:7

   • 2 Timothy 1:14

6. Which of these activities of the Holy Spirit most resonates with you and why?

7. Take a moment to reflect on what you've learned and summarize what you believe about the Holy Spirit.

8. Compare your last answer with the answer you gave to the first question in Lesson 1. What similarities and differences do you see between your answers?

9. How have you applied what you've learned throughout the year, and what difference has it made in your life?

> *"If our culture is to be transformed, it will happen from the bottom up — from ordinary believers practicing apologetics over the backyard fence or around the barbecue grill."*
>
> Charles Colson[50]

Pyro Principles:
What principles did you learn in this week's lesson? Remember, a principle is a truth about God (His person, character, etc.), a promise or warning from God, or a statement of how He relates to mankind.

Are you fired up?
What changes did this week's lesson **spark** in your life?

Fan the Flame
Spend time each day intentionally asking God to help you apply what you've learned in this lesson. Refer to the prayer tips at the beginning of this workbook to provide a framework for your prayer time if you don't already have one. Cultivating a strong prayer life helps you engage the power of the Holy Spirit!

Talk Notes:

"But you, dear friends, by building yourselves up in your most holy faith and praying in the Holy Spirit, keep yourselves in God's love as you wait for the mercy of our Lord Jesus Christ to bring you to eternal life."
Jude 20-21 (NIV)

Notes

[1] Dictionary.com, LLC

[2] Lange, J. P., Schaff, P., Moll, C. B., Briggs, C. A., Forsyth, J., Hammond, J. B., McCurdy, J. F., Conant, T. J. (2008). *A Commentary on the Holy Scriptures: Psalms* (p. 530). Bellingham, WA: Logos Bible Software.

[3] Charles C. Ryrie, *The Holy Spirit* (Chicago: Moody Publishers, 1997), 42.

[4] *The Jeremiah Study Bible: NKJV* (Worthy Publishing, 2013), 207.

[5] *NIV Cultural Backgrounds Study Bible* (Grand Rapids, Michigan: Zondervan, 2016), 763.

[6] *The Jeremiah Study Bible: NKJV* (Worthy Publishing, 2013), 336.

[7] Abraham Kuruvilla, *Judges: A Theological Commentary for Preachers* (Eugene, Oregon: Cascade Books), 224.

[8] *The Jeremiah Study Bible: NKJV* (Worthy Publishing, 2013), 1388.

[9] Billy Graham, *The Holy Spirit* (Nashville, Tennessee: Thomas Nelson, 1988), xvi.

[10] Dr. Thomas L. Constable (Notes on Acts, 2017 Edition, published by Sonic Light: www.soniclight.com)

[11] *The Jeremiah Study Bible: NKJV* (Worthy Publishing, 2013), 1486.

[12] *The Jeremiah Study Bible: NKJV* (Worthy Publishing, 2013), 1494.

[13] *The Jeremiah Study Bible: NKJV* (Worthy Publishing, 2013), 1495.

[14] *The Jeremiah Study Bible: NKJV* (Worthy Publishing, 2013), 1501.

[15] *The Jeremiah Study Bible: NKJV* (Worthy Publishing, 2013), 1507.

[16] *The MacArthur Study Bible, New American Standard Updated Edition* (Nelson Bibles, 2013), 1924-1925.

[17] *Life Application Study Bible: New International Version* (Grand Rapids, Michigan: Zondervan and Carol Stream, Illinois: Tyndale Publishers, Inc., 2007), 1831.

[18] *Life Application Study Bible: New International Version* (Grand Rapids, Michigan: Zondervan and Carol Stream, Illinois: Tyndale Publishers, Inc., 2007), 1835.

[19] Billy Graham, *The Holy Spirit* (Nashville, Tennessee: Thomas Nelson, 1988), 50.

[20] *The Jeremiah Study Bible: NKJV* (Worthy Publishing, 2013), 1445.

[21] Charles C. Ryrie, *The Holy Spirit* (Chicago: Moody Publishers, 1997), 91.

[22] Charles C. Ryrie, *The Holy Spirit* (Chicago: Moody Publishers, 1997), 91.

[23] David Jeremiah, *God in You* (New York: Multnomah Books, 1998), 124-125.

[24] *A Compend of Wesley's Theology*, eds. Burtner and Chiles (Nashville: Abingdon Press, 1954), 95.

[25] David Jeremiah, *God in You* (New York: Multnomah Books, 1998), 128.

[26] Dr. Thomas L. Constable, Notes on Acts, 2017 Edition, published by Sonic Light: www.soniclight.com

[27] David Jeremiah, *God in You* (New York: Multnomah Books, 1998), 84.

[28] Billy Graham, *The Holy Spirit* (Nashville, Tennessee: Thomas Nelson, 1988), 74-75.

[29] Billy Graham, *The Holy Spirit* (Nashville, Tennessee: Thomas Nelson, 1988), 83.

[30] Billy Graham, *The Holy Spirit* (Nashville, Tennessee: Thomas Nelson, 1988), 82.

[31] David Jeremiah, *God in You* (New York: Multnomah Books, 1998), 99.

[32] *Life Application Study Bible: New International Version* (Grand Rapids, Michigan: Zondervan and Carol Stream, Illinois: Tyndale Publishers, Inc., 2007), 1984.

[33] Charles C. Ryrie, *The Holy Spirit* (Chicago: Moody Publishers, 1997), 9.

[34] *NIV Cultural Backgrounds Study Bible* (Grand Rapids, Michigan: Zondervan, 2016), 2054.

[35] *The Jeremiah Study Bible: NKJV* (Worthy Publishing, 2013), 1791.

36 David Jeremiah, *God in You* (New York: Multnomah Books, 1998), 169.

37 David Jeremiah, *God in You* (New York: Multnomah Books, 1998), 173-174.

38 Billy Graham, *The Holy Spirit* (Nashville, Tennessee: Thomas Nelson, 1988), 233.

39 *The Jeremiah Study Bible: NKJV* (Worthy Publishing, 2013), 1542.

40 David Jeremiah, *God in You* (New York: Multnomah Books, 1998), 193-194.

41 Kenneth Boa, "The Gifts of the Spirit," Bible.org, May 11, 2006, https://bible.org/article/gifts-spirit.

42 Richard B. Gaffin et al., *Are Miraculous Gifts for Today?*, ed. Wayne Grudem (Grand Rapids, Michigan: Zondervan, 1996), 10–12.

43 Daniel B. Wallace, *Who's Afraid of the Holy Spirit?* (Dallas, Texas: Biblical Studies Press, 2005), 13.

44 Billy Graham, *The Holy Spirit* (Nashville, Tennessee: Thomas Nelson, 1988), 208.

45 David Jeremiah, *God in You* (New York: Multnomah Books, 1998), 189-190.

46 *Life Application Study Bible: New International Version* (Grand Rapids, Michigan: Zondervan and Carol Stream, Illinois: Tyndale Publishers, Inc., 2007), 2025.

47 Billy Graham, *The Holy Spirit* (Nashville, Tennessee: Thomas Nelson, 1988), 209.

48 Billy Graham, *The Holy Spirit* (Nashville, Tennessee: Thomas Nelson, 1988), 275.

49 Billy Graham, *The Holy Spirit* (Nashville, Tennessee: Thomas Nelson, 1988), xii.

50 Charles Colson, *How Now Shall We Live?* (Tyndale House Publishers, Inc., 2011), 62.

Congratulations!

You have completed this study of God's Holy Spirit – great job! We pray that you have been challenged by what you have learned this year and grown closer to the Lord as you have applied His Word in your life.

It's important that you don't stop now! Here are some suggestions to help you continue to grow:

Daily Prayer: Continue the habit of starting each day with prayer. It's a conversation between you and God. Talk with Him about your day. Praise Him and share your concerns. Ask Him to fill you with His Spirit and guide your decisions each day. Strive to keep Him at the forefront of your thoughts.

Daily Bible Reading: Since you have been studying the early church and the difference the Holy Spirit made in and through the apostles, perhaps you would enjoy reading through some of their teachings such as Paul's epistles and the letters of Peter, James, and John. We would also recommend reading Psalms and Proverbs which are wonderful books full of practical wisdom to apply in your life.

Start Another Study: We have a variety of studies available, including some of Paul's letters as well as an in-depth study on the life of Jesus called ***Mosaic of the Master (volumes I and II)***. There are also a number of excellent Bible studies available at your local Christian bookstore or online. Regardless of which one you select, the important thing is to continue to study His Word!

Visit our Website: There you will find additional studies, tips, encouragement, and resources to help you in your walk with God. Visit our blog for devotionals and announcements, and follow us on Facebook and Twitter for daily encouragement.

Sign-up for Mondays with Mark: Our weekly video devotional will help you begin your week in God's Word. These 2-minute videos arrive in your email inbox every Monday morning. To learn more, visit **www.MondaysWithMark.org**

We would love to hear from you! Please send your thoughts and feedback on this study to us by emailing: **info@lifemarkministries.org**. Share how this study has impacted your life and what you have learned through it.

www.LifeMarkMinistries.org
www.Facebook.com/LifeMarkMinistries
www.Twitter.com/LifeMarkMin

Additional Resources by LifeMark Ministries

On the Pathway with Paul

For centuries, letters have been used to communicate news, pertinent information, and personal stories. Sometimes they express love and joy, and other times they convey desperation and grief. Before the days of telephones and technology, letters were often the only way to converse with family and friends. When received, they were treasured as long-awaited gifts.

So it was with letters authored by the Apostle Paul. His letters to the churches flowed from his heart as he both praised their faithfulness and exhorted them to live lives worthy of the gospel of Jesus Christ.

Our series, *On the Pathway With Paul*, will help you apply Paul's teachings to your life and be transformed by the study of God's Word.

First Step: Laying the Foundation for a God-honoring Life

In any building project, the most critical stage is laying a solid foundation. It is the same for our Christianity, too. If we know the basics of our faith, then we will be able to weather the storms of life.

This 10-week study is designed to ground you in those basics. Whether you are a new believer or someone who has been a Christian for years but wants to review the foundations of your faith, you will find this study to be helpful. The following five topics are covered, with two weeks on each topic: God the Father, The Bible, God the Son, God the Holy Spirit, and The Holy Trinity. For each topic, there will be verses to read, questions to answer, and a summary of the video. The videos are available separately as part of the First Step Leader's Kit.

Mosaic of the Master

Jesus was born. He served. He died and was resurrected.

We all know the basics of the greatest story in history. Most of us have heard the details for years. We celebrate at Christmas and Easter every year, and we often quote famous passages from the Bible.

However, those basics are simply vital pieces in the mosaic of Who Jesus is. The four Gospel authors give a much more in-depth and thorough picture of Jesus — His teachings, His miracles, His submission to the Father, His love and compassion for the least among us, His very heart.

Each piece will show you a different aspect of Jesus through the eyes of Matthew, Mark, Luke, and John. You will be challenged to grow in new ways as you piece together Jesus' story and see the beautiful mosaic God painted of His Son through His Word. ***It will change your own life story!***

Your Purpose Puzzle: Discover Your *Why*

Ponder your life for a moment.

Why are you living in your town? Why do you have the job you have? Why are you in a specific relationship? Why are you living in your current conditions, whatever they might be? God has a purpose for everyone — a purpose that He determined for us before we were even born. He created us specifically for this purpose. We rarely see the full picture, but God gradually reveals pieces of it over time. It is our job to assemble the puzzle and faithfully carry out our purpose. This guide will walk you through the process of prayerfully evaluating your God-given purpose and pursuing it!

Aging with Honor: A Practical Guide to Help You Honor Your Parents as They Age

Growing up is hard to do. That's why God gave kids parents — to teach, train, help, and guide them as they go from having a lot of limitations to having a lot of freedoms and into adulthood.

Growing old is even harder. That's why God gave parents kids — to encourage, support, help, and guide them as they go from having a lot of freedoms to having a lot of limitations.

This practical guide will cover a variety of issues in five individual segments: Financial Needs, Medical Needs, Logistical Needs, Relational Needs, and Spiritual Needs. It will provide you with the tools and resources that you will need in order to evaluate your situation and create a plan that works best for your family.

His House: Renovate Your Life

Do you ever wonder what plans God has for you? Do you question your purpose on earth? Change the way you think, and His plans for your life will unfold before you. That is what His House is designed to do...transform your way of thinking by guiding you through what God has to say about a wide variety of real-life issues. This year-long ONLINE Bible study includes 250-300 short video lessons as well as weekly homework. This study is ideal for people who need to study at their own pace or at unusual times...for the business traveler, the mom, the student — really for anyone! It will focus on tangible, practical principles based on God's Word that help you apply His truth in your life.

To find out more about these and other resources or to place an order, visit our website:

www.LifeMarkMinistries.org

Facebook.com/LifeMarkMinistries   @LifeMarkMin

Mark is available for speaking engagements and conferences. Please contact our office to discuss your event.

www.ingramcontent.com/pod-product-compliance
Lightning Source LLC
Chambersburg PA
CBHW080454170426
43196CB00016B/2793